KNITS THAT *breathe*

12 BREEZY PROJECTS TO KEEP YOU COOL

For my mother, Lily G. Iselin, in gratitude
for passing on her creativity genes.

KNITS THAT *breathe*

12 BREEZY PROJECTS TO KEEP YOU COOL

Julie Turjoman

First Edition ISBN 978-0-9911486-0-8
eISBN 978-0-9911486-1-5
Includes bibliographical references.

Printed in China by Asia Pacific Offset

Published by Passiflora Press/Chicago, IL 60654

Technical editing by Therese Chynoweth
Design, layout, and photography by Zoë Lonergan

www.julieturjoman.com

CONTENTS

The light bulb clicked on for me at one of the many fiber industry events I attend each year. The event convention center seemed to echo with knitters bemoaning the fact that, for a variety of reasons, they could no longer wear their warm and woolly sweaters. Frustration dripped from their voices as perspiration beaded their foreheads, because they suffered from Itchy Wool Syndrome, Acute Tropical Climatitis, or that midlife condition for which time is the only sure antidote, Variable Personal Thermostatosis (known to the rest of the world as 'hot flashes').

This thought occurred to me: perhaps it's no accident that the garment we call a sweater contains the word "sweat."

But there had to be a way for knitters to triumph over these challenges, because we love our sweaters and won't give them up without a fight. While some altruistic souls are content to knit exclusively for others, or to limit their talent to crafting accessories, I freely admit I am not that selfless and neither are most of my knitting friends. Personally, I'd rather make a sweater than any other project.

So, back to that light bulb. Reading about plant and alternative fiber yarns, I was struck by how often their descriptions included words like "non-allergenic," "cooling," "absorbent," "heat-regulating," and "anti-bacterial." But could yarn be all those things? *Really?*

Yes, really. Whatever your reason – life in a warm and humid climate, an unpredictable internal thermostat, or sensitivity to animal fibers – KNITS THAT BREATHE has you covered. Within these pages is a collection of twelve light-as-air, figure flattering, and beautifully draping garments that keep you cool while flaunting your knitting skills. Varied construction techniques, and details such as strategically placed lace or practical pockets, keep the designs engaging but never frustrating.

KNITS THAT BREATHE tells you what you need to know about how these fibers behave (or don't!) in your knitting. And, it includes a dozen patterns for cool tunics, tees, cardigans, shrugs, and tanks that you can wear with comfort and confidence. Now, you can enjoy the supreme comfort and beauty of plant-derived fibers that knitters have always loved, such as cotton, linen, and bamboo – as well as the high-tech benefits of modern alternatives such as soy and milk, Tencel™, Outlast®, and SeaCell®. The forgiving drape and graceful movement of garments knitted from these fibers make them an excellent choice for plus-size bodies. More than half of the projects are sized up to a 54" bust or larger, with special instructions where necessary to achieve optimal fit.

Before you begin knitting any of the projects in this book, make sure you choose the correct size. To ensure the best fit, you are strongly encouraged to make a generous gauge swatch first. This is especially important when working with an unfamiliar fiber or blend. While you undoubtedly have at least basic knitting skills in your toolbox, please visit www.julieturjoman.com for helpful tutorials on unfamiliar techniques.

These patterns have been carefully test-knitted and tech edited for clarity, but despite our best efforts a few errors may occur. If you think you have found a mistake, or have a question about pattern directions, please visit the website for contact information and errata corrections. For help with your project, please join the KNITS THAT BREATHE group on Ravelry. It's a great place to ask questions and share wisdom with other knitters working on the same projects.

FIBER RESOURCE GUIDE

Fiber	Source	Takes dye well/ colorfast	Moisture-wicking	Drape	Hand	Elasticity
Bamboo	Bamboo plant stem; grass family (renewable resource)	Yes	Yes	Excellent	Natural luster; can be softer than silk	Very little; tends to stretch over time. Often blended with wool to allow better shape retention
Cotton	Cotton Plant	Absorbs dye well, but colors will fade over time	Yes	Good	Soft; Combed cotton is especially smooth	Stretches or "grows" over time; often blended with wool to allow better shape retention
Linen	Stem of the Flax Plant	Yes	Yes	Excellent	Crisp; softens with washing and develops a beautiful sheen	None
Milk	Wet-spun Skim Milk (casein) protein	Yes	Yes	Excellent	Soft; luxurious hand resembling cashmere.	Yes
Outlast®	Polyester fiber	Superior	Superior	Good	Soft	Good, when blended with wool
SeaCell®	Powdered Seaweed added to Lyocell (cellulosic fiber)	Superior	Superior	Superior	Soft; lustrous sheen resembling silk.	None
Silk	Silkworms	Yes	Yes	Superior	Variable depending on processing technique; lustrous sheen.	None
Soy	Wet-spun Soybean Protein	Yes	Yes	Good	Soft; sheen similar to silk	Some
Tencel™	Man-made Cellulosic fiber from wood pulp	Superior	Yes	Good	Soft; resistant to wrinkling	Very little; retains appearance after washing, with minimal shrinkage

Antimicrobial/ Antibacterial Properties	Absorbent/ Evaporative	Susceptible to Mildew	Temperature Regulating	Breathability	Blends Well With Other Fibers	Non-allergenic	Strength
Yes	Superior			Yes	Yes	Yes	Resilient, strong fiber
	Dries quickly, highly absorbent	Yes		Yes	Yes		Excellent
	Dries quickly, highly absorbent	Yes		Yes	Yes		Durable, with excellent tensile strength
	Excellent	Yes	Somewhat	Yes	Yes		Highly resilient
	Superior		Superior	Yes	Yes		Highly resilient
Yes, also antifungal and antioxidant	Excellent		Somewhat	Yes	Yes		Good
	Excellent	Yes	Somewhat	Yes	Yes		Excellent
Yes	Excellent		Somewhat	Yes	Yes		Good
	Excellent	Yes		Yes	Yes		Excellent

BREEZY

We all have days when we just don't have the mental bandwidth to put a lot of thought into what to wear. Effortless comfort is key, but pulled-together – even stylish – would be nice, too. So how great is it that organic cotton can be both "green" and chic? Reach for this tank with its body-skimming A-line shape and deep, picot-edged lace hem that flutters with every breeze. On its own, or tossed on over a T-shirt or camisole, it's the perfect blend of comfort and style.

SIZES

XS (S, M, L, XL, XXL, XXXL) to be worn with 2-3 inches positive ease. Finished width at bust = 37 (39 1/2, 43 1/2, 49 1/2, 52 1/2, 57 1/2, 64 1/2)" [94 (100.5, 110.5, 125.5, 133.5, 146, 164) cm] Finished length = 22 1/2 (23, 23 1/2, 24, 25, 25 1/2, 26 1/2)" [57 (58.5, 59.5, 61.5, 63.5, 65, 66) cm]

MATERIALS

Classic Elite Yarns Verde Collection, Seedling [110 yds (100 m)/1.75oz (50 g), 100% organic cotton]. Color: Prune #4595. 7 (7, 8, 9, 10, 10, 11) skeins.
One pair US Size 5 (3.75 mm) needles
One pair US Size 7 (4.5 mm) needles, or size needed to obtain correct gauge
One US Size G-7 (4.5 mm) crochet hook
Stitch markers
Tapestry needle
Waste yarn

GAUGE

17 sts and 27 rows = 4" (10 cm) in St st on larger needles, blocked.

PATTERN NOTES

Worked in two pieces, front and back, this sleeveless garment has a wide lace border edged with Picot CO. Decrease shaping adds a figure-flattering detail to the basic A-line design. Instructions for the lace pattern are provided in both written row-by-row and chart formats. The ribbed texture of the lace leaves provides weight to the garment's hem, helping it hang smoothly on the body. A centered chest pocket repeats the leaf lace motif.

STITCH GUIDE

Picot CO: *CO 5 sts using the Cable method, then BO 2 sts, slip next st on right needle back onto left needle (3 sts now on left needle); rep from * until there are 2 fewer sts on needle than needed, CO 2 more sts.

Ribbed Leaves Lace: Multiple of 16 sts + 17

Row 1 (RS): K2, yo, ssk, [k1, p1] twice, *[k1, p1] twice, k1, k2tog, yo, k3, yo, ssk, [k1, p1] twice; rep from * to last 9 sts, [k1, p1] twice, k1, k2tog, yo, k2.
Rows 2 and 4 (WS): P5, *[k1, p1] 4 times, p9; rep from * to last 12 sts, [k1, p1] 3 times, k1, p5.
Row 3: K1, [yo, ssk] twice, p1, k1, p1, *[k1, p1] twice, [k2tog, yo] twice, k1, [yo, ssk] twice, p1, k1, p1; rep from * to last 9 sts, [k1, p1] twice, [k2tog, yo] twice, k1.
Row 5: K1, yo, p1, ssk, yo, ssk, k1, p1, *k1, p1, k1, k2tog, yo, k2tog, p1, yo, k1, yo, p1, ssk, yo, ssk, k1, p1; rep from * to last 9 sts, k1, p1, k1, k2tog, yo, k2tog, p1, yo, k1.
Row 6: P2, k1, p4, k1, p1, *k1, p4, k1, p3, k1, p4, k1, p1; rep from to last 8 sts, k1, p4, k1, p2.
Row 7: K1, yo, k1, p1, ssk, yo, ssk, p1, *k1, p1, k2tog, yo, k2tog, p1, [k1, yo] twice, k1, p1, ssk, yo, ssk, p1; rep from * to last 9 sts, k1, p1, k2tog, yo, k2tog, p1, k1, yo, k1.
Row 8: [P3, k1] twice, p1, *k1, p3, k1, p5, k1, p3, k1, p1; rep from * to last 8 sts, [k1, p3] twice.
Row 9: K1, yo, p1, k1, p1, ssk, yo, ssk, *k1, k2tog, yo, k2tog, p1, k1, p1, yo, k1, yo, p1, k1, p1, ssk, yo, ssk; rep from * to last 9 sts, k1, k2tog, yo, k2tog, p1, k1, p1, yo, k1.
Row 10: P2, k1, p1, k1, p4, *[p3, k1, p1, k1] twice, p4; rep from * to last 8 sts, p3, k1, p1, k1, p2.
Row 11: K1, yo, [k1, p1] twice, ssk, yo, *sk2p, yo, k2tog, [p1, k1] twice, [yo, k1] twice, p1, k1, p1, ssk, yo; rep from * to last 9 sts, sk2p, yo, k2tog, [p1, k1] twice, yo, k1.

Row 12: [P1, k1] 3 times, p3, *p2, [k1, p1] 5 times, k1, p3; rep from * to last 8 sts, p2, [k1, p1] 3 times.

Row 13: [K1, p1] twice, k1, k2tog, yo, k1, *k2, yo, ssk, [k1, p1] 4 times, k1, k2tog, yo, k1; rep from * to last 9 sts, k2, yo, ssk, [k1, p1] twice, k1.

Row 14: [P1, k1] twice, p5, *p4, [k1, p1] 3 times, k1, p5; rep from * to last 8 sts, p4, [k1, p1] twice.

Row 15: [K1, p1] twice, [k2tog, yo] twice, *k1, [yo, ssk] twice, [p1, k1] 3 times, p1, [k2tog, yo] twice; rep from * to last 9 sts, k1, [yo, ssk] twice, [p1, k1] twice.

Row 16: [P1, k1] twice, p5, *p4, [k1, p1] 3 times, k1, p5; rep from * to last 8 sts, p4, [k1, p1] twice.

Row 17: K1, p1, k1, k2tog, yo, k2tog, p1, yo, *k1, yo, p1, ssk, yo, ssk, [k1, p1] twice, k1, k2tog, yo, k2tog, p1, yo; rep from * to last 9 sts, k1, yo, p1, ssk, yo, ssk, k1, p1, k1.

Row 18: P1, k1, p4, k1, p2, *p1, k1, p4, k1, p1, k1, p4, k1, p2; rep from * to last 8 sts, p1, k1, p4, k1, p1.

Row 19: K1, p1, k2tog, yo, k2tog, p1, k1, yo, *k1, yo, k1, p1, ssk, yo, ssk, p1, k1, p1, k2tog, yo, k2tog, p1, k1, yo; rep from * to last 9 sts, k1, yo, k1, p1, ssk, yo, ssk, p1, k1.

Row 20: P1, [k1, p3] twice, *p2, k1, p3, k1, p1, [k1, p3] twice; rep from * to last 8 sts, p2, k1, p3, k1, p1.

Row 21: K1, k2tog, yo, k2tog, p1, k1, p1, yo, *k1, yo, p1, k1, p1, ssk, yo, ssk, k1, k2tog, yo, k2tog, p1, k1, p1, yo; rep from * to last 9 sts, k1, yo, p1, k1, p1, ssk, yo, ssk, k1.

Row 22: P4, k1, p1, k1, p2, *[p1, k1] twice, p7, k1, p1, k1, p2; rep from * to last 8 sts, [p1, k1] twice, p4.

Row 23: K2tog, yo, k2tog, [p1, k1] twice, yo, *k1, yo, [k1, p1] twice, ssk, yo, sk2p, yo, k2tog, [p1, k1] twice, yo; rep from * to last 9 sts, k1, yo, [k1, p1] twice, ssk, yo, ssk.

Row 24: P3, *[k1, p1] 5 times, k1, p5; rep from * to last 14 sts, [k1, p1] 5 times, k1, p3.

Rep these 24 rows.

DIRECTIONS

BACK

Using smaller needles and Picot method, CO 101 (101, 117, 133, 133, 149, 165) sts.
Work 4 rows in Garter st.
Change to larger needles.
Next (set-up) Row (RS): K2, pm, work Row 1 of Ribbed Leaves lace patt over next 97 (97, 113, 129, 129, 145, 161) sts, pm, k2.
Next Row (WS): K2, sm, work Row 2 of Ribbed Leaves lace patt over next 97 (97, 113, 129, 129, 145, 161) sts, sm k2.
Cont in patt as est until 48 rows (two 24-row rep) have been completed. Piece should meas approx 7½" [19 cm] above Picot CO edge.
Work 4 rows in Garter st, removing markers.
Change to St st and work even for 2" [5 cm], ending with a WS row.

A-line shaping

Next (set up) Row (RS): K15 (15, 18, 22, 22, 25, 30) sts, pm, k71 (71, 81, 89, 89, 99, 105) sts, pm, k15 (15, 18, 22, 22, 25, 30) sts.
Next row: Purl, slipping markers as you come to them.
Next (dec) Row (RS): Knit to marker, sm, ssk, knit to 2 sts before next marker, k2tog, sm, knit to end. 2 sts dec'd.
Rep dec row every 6th row 4 more times, then every 4th row 3 (0, 3, 4, 1, 3, 3) time(s). 85 (91, 101, 115, 121, 133, 149) sts.
Work even until piece meas 16 (16, 16½, 16½, 17, 17, 17)" [40.5 (40.5, 42, 42, 43, 43, 43) cm] above Picot CO edge.

Shape Armholes

BO 3 (3, 4, 4, 5, 6, 8) sts at beg of next 2 rows, then 3 (3, 4, 4, 4, 4, 4) sts at beg of next 2 rows. [73 (79, 85, 99, 103, 113, 125) sts]
Next (dec) row (RS): K2, ssk, knit to last 4 sts, k2tog, k2. [2 sts dec'd]
Rep dec every RS row 2 (1, 3, 3, 3, 3, 3) more time(s). [67 (75, 77, 91, 95, 105, 117) sts]. Work even until armhole meas 6 (6½, 6½, 7, 7½, 8, 8½)" [15 (16.5, 16.5, 18, 19, 20.5, 21.5) cm], ending with a WS.

Right Shoulder

Next Row (RS): K16 (17, 18, 22, 23, 24, 25) sts, turn, leaving rem sts on waste yarn for neck and left shoulder.
Dec 1 st at neck edge every RS row 6 times. [10 (11, 12, 16, 17, 18, 19) sts] rem on needle.
Work 1 WS row even.

Next row (RS): BO 5 (5, 6, 8, 8, 9, 9) sts, knit to end. [5 (6, 6, 8, 9, 9, 10) sts] rem on needle.
Work 1 row even.
BO rem sts.

Left Shoulder

With RS facing, slip last 16 (17, 18, 22, 23, 24, 25) sts to needle, leaving center 35 (41, 41, 47, 49, 57, 67) sts on hold for neck.
Join yarn for a RS row and dec 1 st at neck edge every RS row 6 times. [10 (11, 12, 16, 17, 18, 19) sts] rem on needle.
Next Row (WS): BO 5 (5, 6, 8, 8, 9, 9) sts, purl to end. [5 (6, 6, 8, 9, 9, 10) sts] rem on needle.
Work 1 row even.
BO rem sts.

FRONT

Work Front same as for Back.

POCKET

With smaller needles, CO 24 sts.
Row 1 (RS): Knit.
Row 2: Purl.
Set-up Row: K4, work 16-st rep of Ribbed Leaf Lace over next 16 sts, k4.
Next Row: P4, work 2 of Ribbed Leaf Lace over next 16 sts, p4.
Cont as established through Row 24 of Ribbed Leaf Lace patt, omitting the sk2p on Row 11.
Next Row (RS): Knit.
Next Row: Purl.
BO all sts kwise.

FINISHING

Weave in loose ends.

Block pieces, pinning out the wide lace hem. Sew shoulder seams. Sew side seams from bottom of armhole to top of lace section, leaving lace sections open for greater movement and drape.

With crochet hook and RS facing, work 1 rnd of single crochet around armholes and neck edge, keeping edge smooth. Fasten off.

Sew pocket to front as shown in photo.

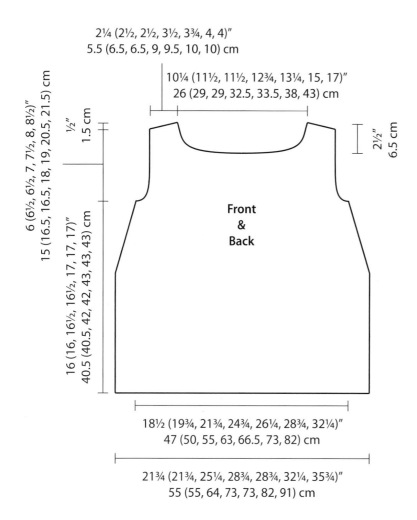

2¼ (2½, 2½, 3½, 3¾, 4, 4)"
5.5 (6.5, 6.5, 9, 9.5, 10, 10) cm

10¼ (11½, 11½, 12¾, 13¼, 15, 17)"
26 (29, 29, 32.5, 33.5, 38, 43) cm

6 (6½, 6½, 7, 7½, 8, 8½)"
15 (16.5, 16.5, 18, 19, 20.5, 21.5) cm

½"
1.5 cm

2½"
6.5 cm

Front
&
Back

16 (16, 16½, 16½, 17, 17, 17)"
40.5 (40.5, 42, 42, 43, 43, 43) cm

18½ (19¾, 21¾, 24¾, 26¼, 28¾, 32¼)"
47 (50, 55, 63, 66.5, 73, 82) cm

21¾ (21¾, 25¼, 28¾, 28¾, 32¼, 35¾)"
55 (55, 64, 73, 73, 82, 91) cm

CHART KEY

☐ k on RS, p on WS

⊡ p on RS, k on WS

⊙ yo

◹ k2tog

◺ ssk

⧄ sk2p

☐ repeat

RIBBED LEAVES LACE

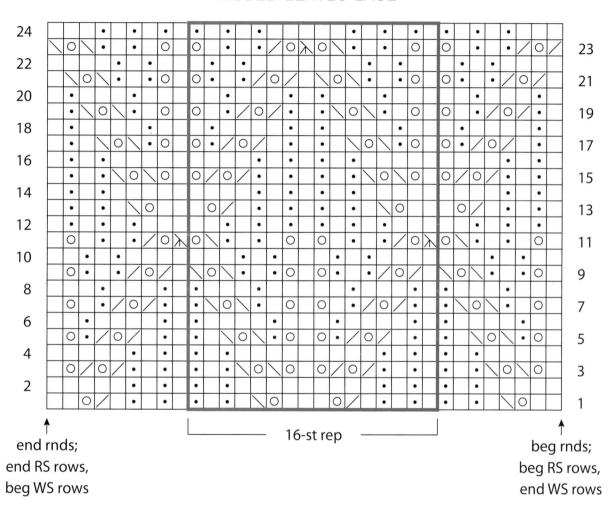

16-st rep

end rnds;
end RS rows,
beg WS rows

beg rnds;
beg RS rows,
end WS rows

FLUTTERBYE

Subtle texture and strategic transparency play well together here, creating a gossamer-light, handkerchief hem top that makes you feel like you're floating on a cool cloud. 100% silk lace yarn glows with a quiet sheen, drapes beautifully, and works up quickly with minimal shaping on mid-sized needles. Sometimes simple luxury is the most elegant.

SIZES
S (M, L, XL) to be worn with 1-2 inches positive ease.
Finished width at bust = 32½ (38, 45¾, 51)" [82.5 (96.5, 116, 129.5) cm]
Finished length = 25½ (26½, 29, 30)" [65 (67.5, 73.5, 76) cm]

MATERIALS
Sundara Silk Lace [1,000 yds (1093 m)/3.5 oz (100 g), 100% silk]. Color: Gingered Peach. 2 (2, 2, 3) skeins.
One US 6 (4 mm) 29" (74 cm) to 36" (91 cm) long circular needle, or size needed to obtain correct gauge
One pair US 7 (4.5 mm) straight needles
One pair US 8 (5 mm) straight needles
Tapestry needle
Stitch markers
Waste yarn or stitch holders
One US F-5 (3.75 mm) crochet hook

GAUGE
21 sts and 34 rows = 4" (10 cm) in St st using 2 strands of yarn held together and US 6 (4 mm) needles.

PATTERN NOTES

The two identical handkerchief hem side panels are knit separately with a single strand of the yarn. The body is knit with two strands of the yarn held together, in two pieces up to the ribcage, at which point the pieces are joined onto one circular needle and knit in the round up to the armholes. From there, the front and back are worked separately. The last few inches are worked with a single strand of yarn. It is important to bind off all pieces very loosely so the yarn doesn't pucker. For those wishing to add a subtly feminine finishing touch, instructions are included for delicate curved ruffles at the neckline and shoulders.

DIRECTIONS

HANDKERCHIEF HEM SIDE PANELS: MAKE TWO.

With US 7 (4.5 mm) needles and one strand of yarn, use Cable method to CO 120 (120, 140, 140) sts. Work in St st until piece meas 10 (10, 12, 12)" [25.5 (25.5, 30.5, 30.5) cm] long. BO loosely with US 8 (5 mm) needles. Set aside.

FRONT

With US 6 (4 mm) needles and 2 strands of yarn held together, use Cable method to CO 100 (115, 135, 145) sts. Work even in St St until piece meas 12 (12, 14, 14)" [30.5 (30.5, 35.5, 35.5) cm] long. Break yarn and place sts on waste yarn or holder, and set aside.

BACK

Work Back the same as for Front until piece meas 12 (12, 14, 14)" [30.5 (30.5, 35.5, 35.5) cm] long. Place Front sts onto same circ needle as Back sts with RS facing out. 200 (230, 270, 290) sts.

Set up rnd: With RS facing, M1L, pm, knit the Front sts, pm, M1R, pm, knit the Back sts. Join to work in the rnd, using a different color marker to indicate beg of rnd. 202 (232, 272, 292) sts. Work 4 rnds even in St st.

A-Line Shaping

Next (dec) rnd: K1, sm, k1, ssk, knit to 3 sts before next marker, k2tog, (k1, sm) twice, k1, ssk, knit to the last 3 sts, k2tog, sm, k1. 4 sts decreased.

Rep dec rnd every 6th rnd 7 (7, 7, 5) times more. 170 (200, 240, 268) sts rem. Work even until body meas 18 (18, 20, 20)" [45.5 (45.5, 51, 51) cm] from bottom edge. Break yarn.

Divide For Armholes

Place 85 (100, 120, 134) sts for Back on holder or waste yarn.

Join 2 strands of yarn to rem sts and work Front back and forth in St st as follows:

Beg with a RS row and BO 3 (4, 6, 7) sts at the beg of next 2 rows, then 2 sts at the beg of next 2 (4, 6, 8) rows. 75 (84, 96, 106) sts rem on needle.

Dec 1 st at each end every other row 2 (3, 6, 7) times. 71 (78, 84, 90) sts rem. Cont even in St st until Front meas 4 (5, 5, 6)" [10 (12.5, 12.5, 15) cm] from beg of armhole. Change to single strand of yarn. Work 1" (2.5 cm) even in St st.

Neck Shaping

Next row (RS): K15 (20, 23, 26) sts, join a 2nd ball of yarn and BO center 41 (38, 38, 38) sts, k15 (20, 23, 26). Work each side separately at the same time. BO at neck edge 2 (3, 3, 4) sts once, then 2 sts 0 (1, 2, 2) time(s).

Dec 1 st at neck edge 3 (3, 2, 2) times as follows: Knit to last 3 sts, ssk, k1; k1, k2tog knit to end. 10 (12, 14, 16) sts rem on needle.

Work even until armhole meas 7½ (8½, 9, 10)" [19 (21.5, 23, 25.5) cm] long. BO rem sts.

Back: Work Back same as for Front.

FINISHING

Sew shoulder seams, being careful not to let sts pucker. Block to finished measurements. Sew handkerchief panels to sides of Front and Back, with side edges of Side Panels even with lower edges of Front and Back, and center of each Side Panel at join of Front and Back.

With US F-5 (3.75 mm) crochet hook and one strand of yarn, work 1 rnd of sc around armholes and neckline to stabilize the edges, being careful to keep the stitches from becoming too tight.

Neckline Ruffle (Optional)

Row 1 (RS): With US 7 (4.5 mm) needles, 1 strand of yarn, and with WS facing, pick up and knit 50 (56, 64, 70) sts along Front neckline, starting and ending 3 (3, 3½, 3½)" [7.5 (7.5, 9, 9) cm] below each shoulder seam.

Row 2: Purl.

Row 3 (inc): K2, [kfb] to last 2 sts, k2. 96 (108, 124, 136) sts.

Row 4: Purl.

Work even in St st for 1" (2.5 cm).

Beg Short-Row Shaping

On next 2 rows, work to last 6 sts, wrap next st and turn. On next 2 rows, work to last 12 sts, wrap next st and turn.

Work 6 more rows as est, working 6 fewer sts before wrapping each time. 36 (48, 64, 76) sts rem in work at center with 30 sts out of work at each end.

Next row (RS): Knit to end, picking up the wraps and working them together with the sts they wrap as you come to them.

Next row (WS): Purl to end, picking up rem wraps and working them together with the sts they wrap.

BO all sts loosely.

Sleeve Cap Ruffles (Optional)

Row 1 (RS): With US 7 (4.5 mm) needles, 1 strand of yarn and with RS facing, pick up and knit 64 (70, 76, 82) sts along outer edge of armhole, starting and ending 4½ (5, 5½, 6)" [11.5 (12.7, 14, 15) cm] below shoulder seam on each side of armhole.

Row 2: Purl.

Row 3 (inc): K2, [kfb] to last 2 sts, k2 124 (136, 148, 160) sts.

Row 4: Purl.

Beg Short-Row Shaping

On next 2 rows, work to last 6 sts, wrap next st and turn. On next 2 rows, work to last 12 sts, wrap and turn.

Work 8 more rows as est, working 6 fewer sts before wrapping each time. 28 (34, 40, 46) rem in work at center with 36 sts out of work at each end.

Next row (RS): Knit to end, picking up the wraps and working them together with the sts they wrap as you come to them.

(WS): Purl to end, picking up rem wraps and working them together with the sts they wrap.

BO all sts loosely.

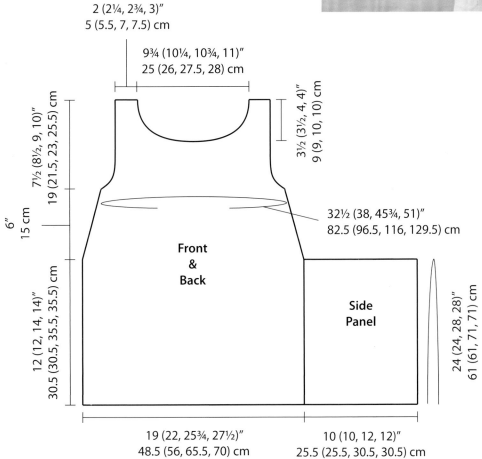

2 (2¼, 2¾, 3)"
5 (5.5, 7, 7.5) cm

9¾ (10¼, 10¾, 11)"
25 (26, 27.5, 28) cm

3½ (3½, 4, 4)"
9 (9, 10, 10) cm

7½ (8½, 9, 10)"
19 (21.5, 23, 25.5) cm

6"
15 cm

32½ (38, 45¾, 51)"
82.5 (96.5, 116, 129.5) cm

Front & Back

Side Panel

12 (12, 14, 14)"
30.5 (30.5, 35.5, 35.5) cm

24 (24, 28, 28)"
61 (61, 71, 71) cm

19 (22, 25¾, 27½)"
48.5 (56, 65.5, 70) cm

10 (10, 12, 12)"
25.5 (25.5, 30.5, 30.5) cm

HAVEN

Simplicity meets sophistication in Haven with its simple two-piece construction and an easily memorized, off-center lace panel. Gentle increasing and short-row shaping add a subtle slope to the shoulders, lending this project its own quiet drama. The cotton and linen blend yarn provides both structure and drape, with softness from the cotton and crisp stitch definition from the linen. In fact, Haven's versatility is one of its most attractive features; it's a poncho, a beach cover-up, or a tunic – you decide. It would be equally attractive and comfortable in 100% cotton, or in bamboo or Tencel for softer drape.

SIZES

XS (S, M, L, XL, XXL, 3XL, 4XL)
Finished width below armholes =
43¼ (47¼, 51¼, 55¼, 59¼, 63¼,
67¼, 71¼)" [110 (120, 132, 140.5,
150.5, 160.5, 171, 181) cm]
To be worn with 4 - 6" [10 – 15 cm]
positive ease.
Length = 23 (23, 24, 24 1/2, 25,
25, 25 1/2, 26)" [58.5 (58.5, 61, 62,
63.5, 63.5, 65, 66) cm]

MATERIALS

Berroco Linsey [114 yds (104
m)/1.75oz (50 g), 64% cotton/36%
linen]. Color: Sycamore #6520. 7 (8,
8, 9, 9, 10, 10, 11) skeins.
One pair US Size 7 (4.5 mm)
needles, or size needed to obtain
gauge
One pair US Size 6 (4 mm) straight
and 16" (40 cm) long circular
needles
Stitch markers
Waste yarn or stitch holders
Tapestry needle

GAUGE

20 sts and 21 rows = 4" (10 cm) in
St st on larger needles, blocked.

PATTERN NOTES

Armhole increases and short-row shaping allow the shoulders to slope down over the upper arm. Lace pattern directions are given in both written row-by-row and chart formats. Haven is worked in two identical pieces from the bottom up, and then seamed together.

STITCH GUIDE

Zig-Zag Lace
(multiple of 12 sts + 1)

Row 1 (RS): K2, *yo, ssk, p4, yo, ssk, k4; rep from * twice more, ending last rep k3.
Row 2 and all other WS rows: Purl.
Row 3: K2, *k1, yo, ssk, p4, yo, ssk, k3; rep from * twice more, ending last rep k2.
Row 5: K2, *k2, yo, ssk, p4, yo, ssk, k2; rep from * twice more, ending last rep k1.
Row 7: K2, *k3, yo, ssk, p4, yo, ssk, k1; rep from * twice more, ending last rep ssk.
Row 9: K2, *k1, k2tog, yo, p4, k2tog, yo, k3; rep from * twice more, ending last rep k2.
Row 11: K2, *k2tog, yo, p4, k2tog, yo, k4; rep from * twice more, ending last rep k3.
Row 13: K1, k2tog, *yo, p4, k2tog, yo, k4, k2tog; rep from * twice more, ending last rep k4.
Row 15: K2tog, yo, *p4, k2tog, yo, k4, k2tog, yo; rep from * twice more, ending last rep k5.
Rep these 16 rows.

DIRECTIONS

FRONT
With smaller straight needles and Cable method, CO 110 (120, 130, 140, 150, 160, 170, 180) sts.
Knit 4 rows.
Change to larger needles.
Set-Up row (RS): K3, pm, k18 (20, 24, 26, 30, 32, 34, 36), pm, work Row 1 of Zigzag Lace pattern over next 37 sts, pm, knit to last 3 sts, pm, k3.
Next row (WS): K3, sm, purl to last 3 sts, slipping markers as you come to them, k3.

Work even until piece meas 6 (6, 6, 6½, 6 ½, 7, 7, 7)" [15 (15, 15, 16.5, 16.5, 18, 18, 18) cm] from CO edge, ending with a WS row.
Next row (RS): K3, remove marker, cont in established patt to last marker, re-move marker, k3.
Next row (WS): Purl.

Cont in St st, work lace patt between markers. Work even until piece meas 12 (12, 12½, 12½, 13, 13½, 14, 14)" [30.5 (30.5, 32, 32, 33, 34.5, 35.5, 35.5) cm] from CO edge, ending with a WS row. Place locking marker in last st at each end of row to mark beg of armholes.

Begin Armhole Shaping
Next (inc) row (RS): K3, pm, M1, work in patt to last 3 sts, M1, pm, k1. 2 sts increased.
Slipping markers as you come to them, work 5 rows even. Rep inc row on next row, then every 6th row 5 more times, working new sts in St st. 124 (134, 144, 154, 164, 174, 184, 194) sts
Cont even until piece meas 20 (20, 21, 21½ , 22, 22, 22½, 23)" [51 (51, 53.5, 54.5, 56, 56, 57, 58.5) cm], ending with a WS row.
Next row (RS): Work 42 (46, 50, 54, 58, 62, 66, 69) in established patt, pm, work 40 (42, 44, 46, 48, 50, 52, 56), pm, k42 (46, 50, 54, 58, 62, 66, 69).

Begin Shoulder Shaping
Cont lace patt and sm as you come to them work short-rows as foll:
Short-row 1 (RS): Work to last 6 sts, wrap next st and turn.
Short-row 2 (WS): Sl 1 purlwise, purl to last 6 sts, wrap next st and turn.
Short-row 3: Sl 1 purlwise, work to last 12 sts, wrap next st and turn.
Short-row 4: Sl 1 purlwise; purl to last 12 sts, wrap next st and turn.
Work 8 (10, 12, 12, 14, 16, 16, 18) more short-rows, working 6 fewer sts before turning each time, ending with a WS row. 52 (50, 48 58, 56, 54, 64, 62) sts rem in work at center
Next row (RS): Work to end, picking up wraps and working them together with the sts they wrap, and remove neck markers. Place 40 (42, 44, 46, 48, 50, 52, 56) center sts on waste yarn for neck. Break yarn.

Join a new ball of yarn and work across other shoulder, picking up wraps and working them together with the sts they wrap. Place rem 42 (46, 50, 54, 58, 62, 66, 69) sts for each shoulder onto waste yarn or spare needles.

BACK
Work Back same as for the Front.

FINISHING
Place sts for each shoulder on separate smaller needles. Holding needles for Front and Back with RS together, and with larger needle, join shoulders using 3-Needle BO.

Neck Edge
With RS facing, place front and back neck sts on circ needle.
Rnd 1: K40 (42, 44, 46, 48, 50, 52, 56) Back neck sts, pick up and k2 sts across gap between Front and Back, k40 (42, 44, 46, 48, 50, 52, 56) Front neck sts, pick up and k2 sts across gap between Front and Back. 84 (88, 92, 96, 100, 104, 108, 116) sts
Purl 1 rnd. Knit 1 rnd. Rep last 2 rnds twice more, then purl 1 rnd.

BO all sts knitwise.

Beginning at top of Garter st side edging, sew side seams to underarm markers, using mattress st.

Weave in loose ends.

Block garment, pinning out lace and smoothing slope of shoulders.

CHART KEY

☐ k on RS, p on WS

⊡ p on RS, k on WS

◉ yo

◩ k2tog

◪ ssk

■ repeat

ZIG-ZAG LACE

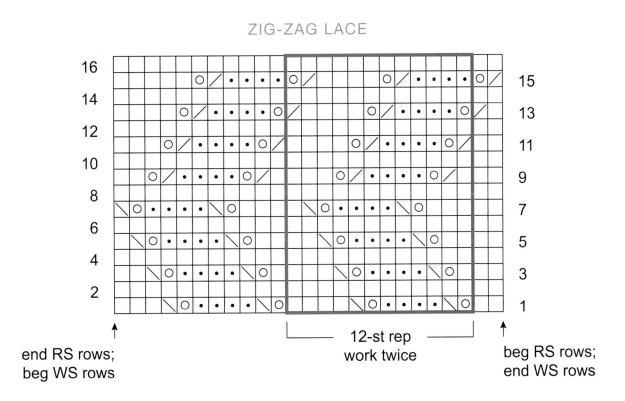

16 · · · 15
14 · · · 13
12 · · · 11
10 · · · 9
8 · · · 7
6 · · · 5
4 · · · 3
2 · · · 1

12-st rep
work twice

end RS rows;
beg WS rows

beg RS rows;
end WS rows

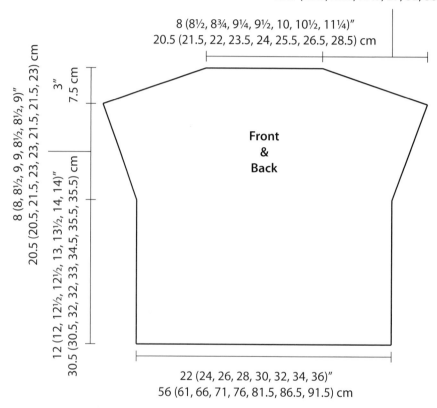

8½ (9¼, 10, 10¾, 11½, 12½, 13¼, 13¾)"
21.5 (23.5, 25.5, 27.5, 29, 32, 33.5, 35) cm

8 (8½, 8¾, 9¼, 9½, 10, 10½, 11¼)"
20.5 (21.5, 22, 23.5, 24, 25.5, 26.5, 28.5) cm

3"
7.5 cm

8 (8, 8½, 9, 9, 8½, 8½, 9)"
20.5 (20.5, 21.5, 23, 23, 21.5, 21.5, 23) cm

12 (12, 12½, 12½, 13, 13½, 14, 14)"
30.5 (30.5, 32, 32, 33, 34.5, 35.5, 35.5) cm

Front & Back

22 (24, 26, 28, 30, 32, 34, 36)"
56 (61, 66, 71, 76, 81.5, 86.5, 91.5) cm

ICED FRAPPUCCINO

It's always summer somewhere, right? When the temperature hits 90 but the heat index and humidity make it feel like 105, nothing cools me down like a tall iced coffee drink. But when there's no caffeine emporium nearby, instead I'll reach for this sleeveless, lacy top with its body-skimming shape and air-conditioned mesh yoke. The unique yarn composition of milk- and soy-based fibers slides softly through the fingers while knitting, and feels heavenly on the body.

SIZES

XS (S, M, L, XL, XXL)
Finished width at bust = 32½ (37¼, 42, 46¾, 54, 58¾)" [82.5 (94.5, 106.5, 118.5, 137, 149) cm]
Finished Length = 23 1/4 (23 1/2, 24 1/4, 26 1/2, 26 3/4, 27 1/4)" [59 (59.5, 61.5, 67.5, 68, 69) cm]

MATERIALS

Kolláge Milky Whey [137 yds (125 m)/1.75oz (50 g), 50% milk, 50% soy). Color: Latte #7608. 6 (7, 7, 8, 9, 9) skeins.
One US 5 (3.75 mm) 24" (60 cm) and 32" (80 cm) circular needles, or size needed to obtain correct gauge.
Tapestry needle
Scrap yarn or stitch holders
Stitch markers in at least two different colors
US F-5 (3.75 mm) crochet hook

GAUGE

approximately 20 sts and 30 rows = 4" (10 cm) in St st, blocked;
24-st Lace Panel = approximately 4¼" (11 cm) wide.

Iced Frappuccino is worked in the round up to the armholes. Then, the Front and Back are worked separately up to the Yoke. The Yoke is worked in the round. Written row-by-row and charted directions are provided for Body lace panel and Yoke.

LACE PANEL (WORKED IN THE ROUND)

(panel of 24 sts)

Rnd 1: K3, k2tog, k4, yo, p2, yo, k2tog, p2, yo, k4, sl 1, k1, psso, k3.
Rnds 2, 4, 6, and 8: K9, p2, k2, p2, k9.
Rnd 3: K2, k2tog, k4, yo, k1, p2, yo, k2tog, yo, p2, k1, yo, k4, sl 1, k1, psso, k2.
Rnd 5: K1, k2tog, k4, yo, k2, p2, yo, k2tog, p2, k2, yo, k4, sl 1, k1, psso, k1.
Rnd 7: K2tog, k4, yo, k3, p2, k2tog, yo, p2, k3, yo, k4, sl 1, k1, psso.
Rep these 8 rnds.

LACE PANEL (WORKED BACK AND FORTH)

(panel of 24 sts)

Row 1 (RS): K3, k2tog, k4, yo, p2, yo, k2tog, p2, yo, k4, sl 1, k1, psso, k3.
Rows 2, 4, 6, and 8: P9, k2, p2, k2, p9.
Row 3: K2, k2tog, k4, yo, k1, p2, yo, k2tog, yo, p2, k1, yo, k4, sl 1, k1, psso, k2.
Row 5: K1, k2tog, k4, yo, k2, p2, yo, k2tog, p2, k2, yo, k4, sl 1, k1, psso, k1.
Row 7: K2tog, k4, yo, k3, p2, k2tog, yo, p2, k3, yo, k4, sl 1, k1, psso.
Rep these 8 rows.

MESH STITCH (WORKED IN THE ROUND)

(multiple of 2 sts)

Rnd 1: K1, *yo, k2tog; rep from * to last st, k1.
Rnds 2 and 4: Knit.
Rnd 3: K2, *yo, k2tog; rep from * to end.
Rep these 4 rnds.

DIRECTIONS

BODY

With longer circ needle, CO 216 (240, 264, 288, 324, 348) sts.
Row 1 (WS): *K1, p1; rep from * to end.
Row 2 (RS): *P1, k1; rep from * to end.
Rows 3 and 4: Rep Rows 1 and 2. Do not turn at end of last row. Pm for beg of rnd and join to work in the rnd, taking care not to twist sts.
Set-Up Rnd: *K6 (10, 14, 18, 22, 26), pm, p3 (3, 3, 3, 4, 4), work Rnd 1 of Lace Panel Chart over next 24 sts, p3 (3, 3, 3, 4, 4), pm; rep from * 5 times more.
Cont as est for 31 (31, 39, 39, 47, 47) more rnds.

Next (dec) rnd: *K2 (4, 6, 8, 10, 12), k2tog, k2 (4, 6, 8, 10, 12), p3, work next rnd of Lace Panel Chart over next 24 sts, p3; rep from * 5 times more. 210 (234, 258, 282, 318, 342) sts rem.

Work 15 rnds even.

Next (dec) rnd: *K2 (4, 6, 8, 10, 12), k2tog, k1 (3, 5, 7, 9, 11), p3, work next rnd of Lace Panel Chart over next 24 sts, p3; rep from * 5 times more. 204 (228, 252, 276, 312, 336) sts rem.

Work 15 rnds even.

Next (dec) rnd: *K1 (3, 5, 7, 9, 11), k2tog, k1 (3, 5, 7, 9, 11), p3, work next rnd of Lace Panel Chart over next 24 sts, p3; rep from * 5 times more. 198 (222, 246, 270, 306, 330) sts rem.

Work 7 rnds even.

Next (dec) rnd: *K0 (2, 4, 6, 8, 10), k2tog, k1 (3, 5, 7, 9, 11), p3, work next rnd of Lace panel Chart over next 24 sts, p3; rep from * 5 times more. 192 (216, 240, 264, 300, 324) sts rem.

Work 7 rnds even.

Next (dec) rnd: *K0 (2, 4, 6, 8, 10), k2tog, k0 (2, 4, 6, 8, 10), p3, work next rnd of Lace Panel Chart over next 24 sts, p3; rep from * 5 times more. 186 (210, 234, 258, 294, 318) sts rem.

Sizes L (XL, XXL) only

Work 7 rnds even.

Next (dec) rnd: *K5 (7, 9), k2tog, k6 (8, 10), p3, work next rnd of Lace Panel Chart over next 24 sts; rep from * 5 times more. 252 (288, 312) sts rem.

All sizes

Work even until body meas 15 (15, 15, 16, 16, 16)" [38 (38, 38, 40.5, 40.5, 40.5) cm].

Next (inc) rnd: *K1 (3, 5, 6, 8, 10), M1, k0 (2, 4, 6, 8, 10), p3, work next rnd of Lace Panel Chart over next 24 sts, p3; rep from * 5 times more. 192 (216, 240, 258, 294, 318) sts.

Sizes L (XL, XXL) only

Work 7 rnds even.

Next (inc) rnd: *K7 (9, 11), M1, k6 (8, 10), p3, work next rnd of Lace Panel Chart over next 24 sts, p3; rep from * 5 times more. 264 (300, 324) sts.

All sizes

Work even until piece meas approx 16 (16, 16, 18, 18, 18)" [40.5 (40.5, 40.5, 45.5, 45.5, 45.5) cm], ending with a completed rep.

DIVIDE FOR ARMHOLES
FRONT

Row 1 (RS): K0 (3, 4, 5, 7, 9) sts, BO 2 (2, 2, 3, 3, 3), work in est patt until there are 94 (106, 118, 129, 147, 159) sts are on right needle. Place rem 96 (108, 120, 132, 150, 162) sts on waste yarn for back, and turn. Beg working back and forth.

Row 2 (WS): BO 2 (2, 2, 3, 3, 3), work to end of row. 92 (104, 116, 126, 144, 156) sts.

Next row (dec, RS): Sl 1, k2tog (or p2tog to maintain patt), work to last 3 sts, ssk (or ssp to maintain patt), k1. 2 sts dec'd.

Next row (WS): Sl 1, work in est patt to end.

Rep these last 2 rows 2 times more. Work even for 8 (8, 8, 16, 16, 16) more rows. 86 (98, 110, 120, 138, 150) sts rem. Place sts on waste yarn.

BACK

Replace held 96 (108, 120, 132, 150, 162) Back sts on longer circ needle. Join yarn and beg working back and forth with a RS row.

BO 2 (2, 2, 3, 3, 3) sts at beg of next 2 rows. Complete Back same as Front. 86 (98, 110, 120, 138, 150) sts rem. Replace held Front sts on same needle.

YOKE

Notes: When decreasing to shape the yoke over the Diagonal Mesh Stitch, work the k2tog but not the following yarn over for each stitch to be decreased. Use removable markers to mark front, back and shoulders, and move markers up as you work; the Diagonal Mesh St should repeat smoothly around the yoke and space decreases as evenly as possible between markers.

Set-Up row (RS): Turn work with WS facing, and using Cable method, CO 40 (42, 48, 52, 54, 58) sts for shoulder cap, turn work, pm, work Front sts in est patt, pm, turn work with

WS facing and using Cable method, CO 40 (42, 48, 52, 54, 58) sts for shoulder cap, turn work, pm, work across Back sts, pm in different color to mark beg of rnd and join to work in the rnd. 252 (280, 316, 344, 384, 416) sts.

Next rnd: *Work Diagonal Mesh St over 40 (42, 48, 52, 54, 58) shoulder cap sts, sm, work Seed St to next marker, sm; rep from * once more.

Next (dec) rnd: *Work to marker in est patt, sm, dec 0 (4, 4, 8, 8, 12) sts evenly spaced to next marker by working (k2tog, p2tog) for each 2 sts dec'd, sm; rep from * once more. 252 (272, 308, 328, 368, 392) sts rem. Work 2 rnds even.

Next (dec) rnd: *Work to marker in est patt, sm, work in Diagonal Mesh St and dec 6 sts evenly spaced to next marker, sm; rep from * once more. 240 (260, 296, 316, 356, 380) sts rem.

Cont even as est until yoke meas 1 (1, 1½, 1½, 2, 2)" [2.5 (2.5, 4, 4, 5, 5) cm].

Next (dec) rnd: *Work to marker in est patt, sm, work in Mesh St to next marker and dec 6 sts evenly spaced, sm; rep from * once more. 228 (248, 284, 304, 344, 368) sts rem. Work 4 rnds even in Mesh St.

Next (dec) rnd: *Work in est patt to marker and dec 3 (3, 3, 2, 2, 2) sts evenly spaced to next marker, sm, work in est patt and dec 8 sts evenly spaced to next marker, sm; rep from * once more. 206 (226, 262, 284, 324, 348) sts.

Rep last 5 rnds 3 (3, 4, 5, 7, 7) times more, then rep dec rnd once more. 118 (138, 152, 164, 164, 188) sts; 34 (42, 46, 44, 46, 54) sts rem each for Front and Back, and 25 (27, 30, 38 36, 40) sts rem for each shoulder. BO all sts knitwise.

FINISHING

Weave in loose ends.

Wet block tunic, pinning hem straight and sides into an A-Line shape, and shape yoke into a gentle curve.

Edging

With crochet hook and RS facing, work 1 rnd of single crochet around armholes and neckline to stabilize. If the neckline seems a bit loose, work single crochet into 3 of every 4 sts along the BO edge to tighten.

CHART KEY

- ☐ k on RS, p on WS
- ⊡ p on RS, k on WS
- ⊙ yo
- ╱ k2tog
- ⊠ sl 1, k1, psso
- ☐ repeat

MESH LACE

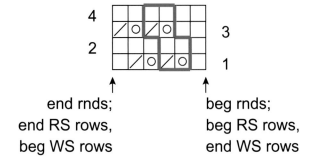

end rnds;
end RS rows,
beg WS rows

beg rnds;
beg RS rows,
end WS rows

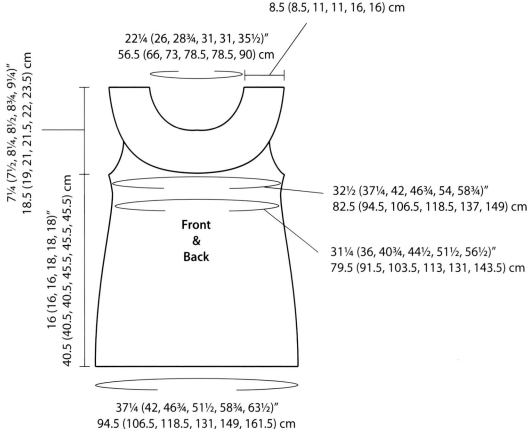

3¼ (3¼, 4¼, 4¾, 6¼, 6¼)"
8.5 (8.5, 11, 11, 16, 16) cm

22¼ (26, 28¾, 31, 31, 35½)"
56.5 (66, 73, 78.5, 78.5, 90) cm

7¼ (7½, 8¼, 8½, 8¾, 9¼)"
18.5 (19, 21, 21.5, 22, 23.5) cm

32½ (37¼, 42, 46¾, 54, 58¾)"
82.5 (94.5, 106.5, 118.5, 137, 149) cm

Front & Back

31¼ (36, 40¾, 44½, 51½, 56½)"
79.5 (91.5, 103.5, 113, 131, 143.5) cm

16 (16, 16, 18, 18, 18)"
40.5 (40.5, 40.5, 45.5, 45.5, 45.5) cm

37¼ (42, 46¾, 51½, 58¾, 63½)"
94.5 (106.5, 118.5, 131, 149, 161.5) cm

BODY LACE PANEL

Note: When working in the round,
read all chart rows from right to left;
when working back and forth,
read RS rows from right to left,
and WS rows from left to right.

PACIFIC COAST

A unique construction technique features a short-row shaped side hem, raised seams, and graduated horizontal stripes that add up to a textured sleeveless tunic with figure-flattering architectural lines. Small decorative buttons are stitched into place to create attractive inverted pleats. Tencel tape yarn glides smoothly through the fingers, creating a soft garment that skims the body with beautiful drape and cool comfort.

SIZES

XS (S, M, L, XL, XXL, XXXL)
Finished width at bust = 33½ (36¾, 40¾, 44¾, 48, 52½, 56)" [85 (93.5, 103.5, 113.5, 122, 133.5, 142) cm]
Finished width at hips = 41½ (44¾, 48¾, 52¾, 56, 60½, 64)" [105.5 (113.5, 124, 134, 142, 153.5, 162.5) cm]
Tunic is designed to be worn with 2" of positive ease. Tunic shown measures 36¾" (93.5 cm).

MATERIALS

Prism Tencel Tape [100% Tencel™; 120 yds [110 m]/2 oz (56 g)]: Color #312. 8 (8, 9, 9, 10, 11, 12) skeins".
US 8 (5 mm) 29" (74 cm) or longer circular and set of 4 or 5 double-pointed needles, or size needed to obtain correct gauge
US 8 (5 mm) straight needles, or size needed to obtain correct gauge, optional
Stitch markers
Four stitch holders
Tapestry needle
US G-6 (4 mm) crochet hook
Five ½" (13 mm) diameter decorative buttons.

GAUGE

20 sts and 26 rows = 4" (10 cm) in St st, blocked.

PATTERN NOTES

The tunic is worked in four pieces. Two center panels (front and back) are identical except in length. Each side panel is worked to the armhole in one piece, then divided and worked back and forth from the armhole to the shoulder. Raised seams add a decorative element.

The tunic's center panels form the inside of both front and back pleats, and include basic shaping. Tunic sides include short-row hem shaping as well as decrease shaping from hip to bust.

STITCH GUIDE

BROKEN STOCKINETTE STITCH
(any number of sts)
Slipping the first st of every row purlwise throughout, beg with a WS row and work 12 rows of St st.
Next row (WS): Knit.
Work 7 rows of St st.
Next row (WS): Knit.
Rep the last 8 rows 1 (1, 1, 2, 2, 2) time(s) more.
Work 5 rows of St st.
Next row (WS): Knit.
Rep the last 6 rows 7 (7, 7, 7, 7, 8) times more.
Work 3 rows of St st.
Next row (WS): Knit.
Rep the last 4 rows to the end.

DIRECTIONS

CENTER FRONT PANEL
With circ or straight needles, CO 32 (34, 40, 44, 48, 51, 56) sts.
Row 1 (RS): Purl.
Row 2 (WS): Knit.
Row 3: Purl.
Beg Broken Stockinette St and AT THE SAME TIME, when panel meas 4" (10 cm), dec on next RS row, then on RS rows every 3" (7.5 cm) 4 times more as foll: Sl 1, k1, ssk, knit to last 4 sts, k2tog, k2. 22 (24, 30, 34, 38, 41, 46) sts rem. Work even in est patt until panel meas 22 (23, 23½, 24, 25, 25½, 26)" [56 (58.5, 59.5, 61, 63.5, 65, 66) cm], ending with a RS row. BO all sts knitwise on WS.

CENTER BACK PANEL

Work same as for Center Front Panel, working even until panel meas 24 (25, 26, 26, 27½, 28, 28½)" [61 (63.5, 66, 66, 70, 71, 72.5) cm], ending with a RS row. BO all sts knitwise on WS.

LEFT SIDE PANEL

With circ needle, CO 76 (82, 86, 92, 96, 104, 108) sts.
Row 1 (RS): Purl.
Row 2 (WS): Knit.
Row 3: Purl.
Row 4: P38 (41, 43, 46, 48, 52, 54) sts, pm to mark center of panel, purl to end.

Begin Short-row Hem Shaping as follows:

Row 5 (RS): Knit to m, sm, k5, w&t.
Row 6 (WS): P10, w&t.
Row 7: Knit to wrapped st, work wrap together with wrapped st, k3, w&t.
Row 8: Purl to next wrapped st, work wrap together with wrapped st, p3, w&t.
Rows 9 – 18: Rep Rows 7 and 8 five times more.
Row 19: Purl to end of row, working the last wrap together with wrapped st.
Work 8 more rows in St st.
Beg with first WS knit row, cont in Broken Stockinette St and AT THE SAME TIME, when panel meas 4" (10 cm) from CO edge along side of panel, dec on next RS row, then on RS rows every 3" (7.5 cm) 4 times more as foll: Knit to 3 sts before marker, ssk, k1, sm, k1, k2tog, knit to end. Note: Dec should match those on front/back center panels. 66 (72, 76, 82, 86, 94, 98) sts rem.
Cont even until panel meas 21 (21½, 22, 22, 23, 23, 23½)" [53.5 (54.5, 56, 56, 58.5, 58.6, 59.5) cm] from CO edge along center of panel, ending with a WS row.

Divide For Armhole

Next row (RS): K31 (34, 35, 38, 39, 43, 44), BO center 4 (4, 6, 6, 8, 8, 10) sts, knit to end. Place first 31 (34, 35, 38, 39, 43, 44) sts on holder, and cont on rem 31 (34, 35, 38, 39, 43, 44) sts.

Left Front

Cont in est patt and BO at armhole edge 2 sts 1 (1, 1, 2, 2, 2, 2) time(s), then dec 1 st at armhole edge every 4th row 4 (4, 4, 5, 5, 5, 4) times. AT THE SAME TIME, when armhole meas 3 (3 1/2, 3 1/2, 4, 4, 4 1/2, 4 1/2)" [7.5 (9, 9, 10, 10, 11.5) cm], end with a RS row.

Front Neck Shaping

BO at beg of WS rows 2 (3, 3, 3, 3, 3, 3) sts 5 (4, 4, 4, 4, 4, 4) times. Dec 1 st at neck edge every 4th row 3 (2, 3, 3, 2, 4, 5) times. 12 (14, 14, 14, 16, 18, 19) sts rem.
Work even until armhole meas 7 (7½, 8, 8½, 9, 9½)" [18 (19, 20.5, 21.5, 23, 24, 25.5) cm]. Place rem sts onto holder.

Left Back

Return held back sts to needles and shape armhole same as front. 25 (28, 29, 29, 30, 34, 36) sts. Work even until armhole meas 5 (5½, 6, 6½, 7, 7½, 7)" [12.5 (14, 15, 16.5, 18, 19, 18) cm], ending with a WS row.

Back Neck Shaping

BO at beg of RS rows 4 (4, 5, 4, 4, 5, 5) sts 2 times, then 3 sts 1 time. Dec 1 st at neck edge 2 (3, 2, 4, 3, 3, 4) times. 12 (14, 14, 14, 16, 18, 19) sts rem.
Work even until armhole meas 7 (7½, 8, 8½, 9, 9½)" [18 (19, 20.5, 21.5, 23, 24, 25.5) cm]. Place rem sts onto holder.

RIGHT SIDE PANEL

Work Right Side Panel same as Left Side Panel to the armhole.
Next row (RS): K31 (34, 35, 38, 39, 43, 44), BO center 4 (4, 6, 6, 8, 8, 10) sts, knit to end. Place first 31 (34, 35, 38, 39, 43, 44) sts on holder, and cont on rem 31 (34, 35, 38, 39, 43, 44) sts.

Right Back

Cont in est patt and BO at armhole edge 2 sts 1 (1, 1, 2, 2, 2, 2) time(s), then dec 1 st at armhole edge every 4th row 4 (4, 4, 5, 5, 5, 4) times. 25 (28, 29, 29, 30, 34, 36) sts rem.

Work even until armhole meas 5 (5½, 6, 6½, 7, 7½, 7)"
[12.5 (14, 15, 16.5, 18, 19, 18) cm], ending with a RS row.

Back Neck Shaping

BO at beg of WS rows 4 (4, 5, 4, 4, 5, 5) sts 2 times, then
3 sts 1 time. Dec 1 st at neck edge 2 (3, 2, 4, 3, 3, 4) times.
12 (14, 14, 14, 16, 18, 19) sts rem.
Work even until armhole meas 7 (7½, 8, 8½, 9, 9½)"
[18 (19, 20.5, 21.5, 23, 24, 25.5) cm]. Place rem sts
onto holder.

Right Front

Return held back sts to needles and shape armhole same
as back. AT THE SAME TIME, when armhole meas 3 (3 1/2,
3 1/2, 4, 4, 4 1/2, 4 1/2)" [7.5 (9, 9, 10 10, 11.5, 11.5) cm],
end with a WS row.

Front Neck Shaping

BO at beg of RS rows 2 (3, 3, 3, 3, 3, 3) sts 5 (4, 4, 4, 4,
4) times. Dec 1 st at neck edge every 4th row 3 (2, 3, 3, 2,
4, 5) times. 12 (14, 14, 14, 16, 18, 19) sts rem.
Work even until armhole meas 7 (7½, 8, 8½, 9, 9½, 10)"
[18 (19, 20.5, 21.5, 23, 24, 25.5) cm]. Place rem sts
onto holder.

FINISHING

Weave in ends. Block pieces to finished measurements.
Sew panels together with seams on RS. Join shoulder
seams using 3-Needle BO, with RS together.

Center Front and Back Pleats

Fold and pin Center Front Panel edges toward center to
form an open pleat, leaving approx 1½ (2, 2, 2½, 2½, 3, 3)"
[4 (5, 5, 6.5, 6.5, 7.5, 7.5) cm] of the center panel exposed.
Fold and pin Center Back Panel so the edges meet at the
center to form a closed pleat.
With crochet hook, work 1 rnd of single crochet around
neck edge, working through all layers of pleats, adjusting
tension of rnd to tighten and neaten neckline. Join with a
slip st in the first st, then fasten off.
Beg at bottom of armhole and work 1 rnd of single crochet
around each armhole. Join with a slip st in the first st, then
fasten off.

Sew buttons to Front and Back pleats as shown in accompanying photos. Secure pleats by stitching buttons firmly
into place through all layers of tunic.

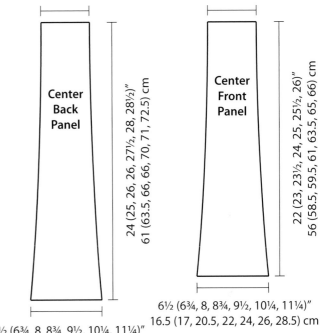

4½ (4¾, 6, 6¾, 7½, 8¼, 9¼)"
11.5 (12, 15, 17, 19, 21, 23.5) cm

4½ (4¾, 6, 6¾, 7½, 8¼, 9¼)"
11.5 (12, 15, 17, 19, 21, 23.5) cm

Center Back Panel

Center Front Panel

24 (25, 26, 26, 27½, 28, 28½)"
61 (63.5, 66, 66, 70, 71, 72.5) cm

22 (23, 23½, 24, 25, 25½, 26)"
56 (58.5, 59.5, 61, 63.5, 65, 66) cm

6½ (6¾, 8, 8¾, 9½, 10¼, 11¼)"
16.5 (17, 20.5, 22, 24, 26, 28.5) cm

6½ (6¾, 8, 8¾, 9½, 10¼, 11¼)"
16.5 (17, 20.5, 22, 24, 26, 28.5) cm

3¼ (3¼, 3½, 4¾, 5¼, 5¼, 5¼)"
8.5 (8.5, 9, 12, 13.5, 13.5, 13.5) cm

2½ (2¾, 2¾, 2¾, 3¼, 3½, 3¾)"
6.5 (7, 7, 7, 8.5, 9, 9.5) cm

2½ (2¾, 2¾, 2¾, 3¼, 3½, 3¾)"
6.5 (7, 7, 7, 8.5, 9, 9.5) cm

2½ (2¾, 3, 3, 2¾, 3¼, 3½)"
6.5 (7, 7.5, 7.5, 7, 8.5, 9) cm

2½ (2¾, 3, 3, 2¾, 3¼, 3½)"
6.5 (7, 7.5, 7.5, 7, 8.5, 9) cm

4 (4, 4½, 4½, 5, 5, 5½)"
10 (10, 11.5, 11.5, 12.5, 12.5, 14) cm

2 (2, 2, 2½, 2½, 2½, 3)"
5 (5, 5, 6.5, 6.5, 6.5, 7.5) cm

7 (7½, 8, 8½, 9, 9½, 10)"
18 (19, 20.5, 21.5, 23, 24, 25.5) cm

24 (25, 26, 26, 27½, 28, 28½)"
61 (63.5, 66, 66, 70, 71, 72.5) cm

22 (23, 23½, 24, 25, 25½, 26)"
56 (58.5, 59.5, 61, 63.5, 65, 66) cm

**Right/ Left
Side
Panel**

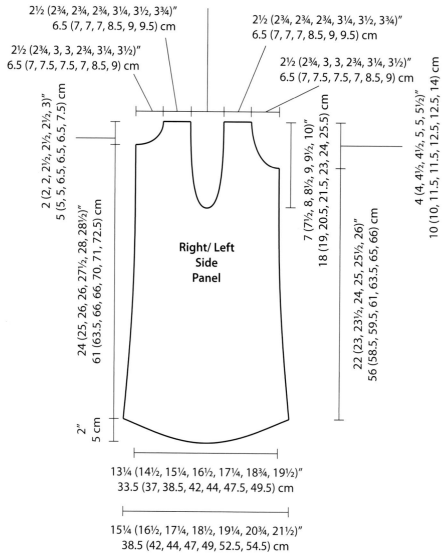

2"
5 cm

13¼ (14½, 15¼, 16½, 17¼, 18¾, 19½)"
33.5 (37, 38.5, 42, 44, 47.5, 49.5) cm

15¼ (16½, 17¼, 18½, 19¼, 20¾, 21½)"
38.5 (42, 44, 47, 49, 52.5, 54.5) cm

POCHETTE

From the French word for "little pocket," this cleverly constructed, body-skimming tunic features vibrant color-blocking in the form of wrap-around, curved pockets. Gentle waist shaping and contrast color piping give Pochette the long, lean lines that flatter a variety of figures. 100% linen yarn provides a crisp hand and nearly weightless drape, two elements that work hard to keep you cool.

SIZES
XS (S, M, L, XL, XXL)
Finished bust circumference= 34
(38, 43½, 49, 55¾, 60¼)" [86.5
(96.5, 110.5, 124.5, 141.5, 153) cm]
Finished length= 26 (26½, 26½,
27, 27, 27½)" [66 (67.5, 67.5, 68.5,
68.5, 70) cm]

MATERIALS
Shibui Linen [246 yds (225 m) /
1.75oz (50 g), 100% linen].
Main Color (MC): Tar #11. 4 (4, 5, 5,
6, 6) skeins.
Contrast Color (CC): Apple #103. 1
(1, 1, 1, 2, 2) skein(s).
One US Size 5 (3.75 mm) 16"
(40 cm), and 29" (74 cm) circular
needles and one set of 4 or 5
double-pointed needles, or size
needed to obtain correct gauge
Stitch markers
Tapestry needle

GAUGE
23 sts and 31 rows = 4" (10 cm) in
St st, blocked 4¼".

PATTERN NOTES

Pochette is worked back and forth from the bottom up, in pieces, which are then seamed. Color-blocking and Reverse Stockinette edging in a contrast color yarn adds visual shaping and definition. Curved pockets are worked along with Back, and are then wrapped around and seamed to the Front of the tunic. The deep V-neck is split at the same level as the beginning of the armhole bind-off. Set-in sleeves are worked seamlessly down from the shoulders, using short-rows to shape the sleeve cap, and then knit in the round down to the Reverse Stockinette edging.

DIRECTIONS

BACK AND POCKETS
With CC and longer circ needle, CO 172 (183, 199, 217, 236, 251) sts using an elastic CO.
Row 1 (RS): Purl.
Row 2 (WS): Knit.
Rep Rows 1 and 2 once more.

Work even in St st until piece meas 4 (4, 4½, 4½, 5, 5)" [10 (10, 11.5, 11.5, 12.5, 12.5) cm] from beg, ending with a WS row.

Right Pocket shaping
Short-Row 1 (RS): K27, wrap & turn.
Short-Rows 2, 4, 6, 8, 10, 12, 14, and 16 (WS): Purl to end.
Short-Row 3: K24, w&t.
Short-Row 5: K21, w&t.
Short-Row 7: K18, w&t.
Short-Row 9: K15, w&t.
Short-Row 11: K12, w&t.
Short-Row 13: K9, w&t.
Short-Row 15: K6, w&t.
Next Row (RS): K36 (36, 38, 40, 42, 44) sts, picking up the wraps and working them with the sts they wrap, pm, knit to end.

Left Pocket shaping
Short-Row 1 (WS): P27, wrap & turn.
Short-Rows 2, 4, 6, 8, 10, 12, 14, and 16 (RS): Knit to end.
Short-Row 3: P24, w&t.
Short-Row 5: P21, w&t.
Short-Row 7: P18, w&t.

Short-Row 9: P15, w&t.
Short-Row 11: P12, w&t.
Short-Row 13: P9, w&t.
Short-Row 15: P6, w&t.
Next row (WS): P36 (36, 38, 40, 42, 44), picking up the wraps and working them with the sts they wrap, pm, purl to end.
Next row (RS): P36 (36, 38, 40, 42, 44), sm, knit to next marker, sm, p36 (36, 38, 40, 42, 44).
Next row (WS): K36 (36, 38, 40, 42, 44), sm, purl to next marker, sm, k36 (36, 38, 40, 42, 44).
Rep these 2 rows once more.
Next row (RS): BO 36 (36, 38, 40, 42, 44) sts, remove marker, knit to end. 136 (147, 161, 177, 194, 207) sts rem on needle.
Next row (WS): BO 36 (36, 38, 40, 42, 44) sts, remove marker, purl to end. 100 (111, 123, 137, 152, 163) sts rem on needle.
Change to MC. Work in St st for 1" [2.5 cm], ending with a WS row.

Waist Shaping

Next (dec) row (RS): K26 (28, 28, 32, 34, 36), pm, ssk, k44 (51, 63, 69, 80, 87) sts, k2tog, pm, knit to end. 2 sts decreased.
Work 3 rows even.
Next (dec) row: Knit to marker, sm, ssk, knit to 2 sts before next m, k2tog, sm, knit to end. [2 sts dec'd]
Rep dec row every 4th row 9 (10, 8, 7, 5, 4) more times, slipping markers as you come to them. 78 (87, 103, 119, 138, 151) sts rem on needle.

Work even until piece meas 11 (11½, 11½, 11½, 11½, 11½)" [28 (29, 29, 29, 29, 29) cm] from beg, ending with a WS row.

Next (inc) row (RS): Knit to marker, sm, M1R, knit to marker, M1L, sm, knit to end. 2 sts increased
Rep inc row every 4th row 10 (12, 11, 11, 10, 10) more times, slipping markers as you come to them. 100 (111, 127, 143, 160, 173) sts rem on needle.
Work even until piece meas 18 (18, 17½, 17½, 17, 17)"

[45.5 (45.5, 44.5, 44.5, 43, 43) cm] from beg, ending with a WS row.

Shape Armholes

BO 4 (4, 4, 6, 7, 7) sts at beg of next 2 rows, then 2 (2, 3, 3, 3, 3) sts at beg of next 2 (2, 4, 4, 6, 6) rows. 88 (99, 107, 119, 128, 141) sts rem on needle.
Next (dec) row (RS): K2, ssk, knit to last 4 sts, k2tog, k2 2 sts decreased.
Rep dec row every RS row 4 (6, 6, 8, 8, 10) more times. 78 (85, 93, 101, 110, 119) sts rem on needle.
Work even until armhole meas 7 (7½, 8, 8½, 9, 9½)" [18 (19, 20.5, 21.5, 23, 24) cm], ending with a WS row.

Shape Neck and Shoulders

Short-Row 1 (RS): K19 (22, 23, 25, 26, 28) sts, join a second ball of yarn and BO center 40 (41, 47, 51, 58, 63) sts for neck, knit to last 4 (5, 5, 6, 6, 6) sts, w&t.
Short-Row 2 (WS): Purl to neck edge; purl to last 4 (5, 5, 6, 6, 6) sts, w&t.
Short-Row 3: Knit to 2 sts before neck edge, k2tog; ssk, knit to last 8 (10, 10, 11, 12, 12) sts, w&t.
Short-Row 4: Purl to neck edge; purl to last 8 (10, 10, 11, 12, 12) sts, w&t.
Short-Row 5: Knit 2 sts before neck edge, k2tog; ssk, knit to last 12 (14, 15, 16, 17, 18) sts, w&t.
Short-Row 6: Purl to neck edge; purl to last 12 (14, 15, 16, 17, 18) sts, w&t.
Short-Row 7: Knit to 2 sts before neck edge, k2tog; ssk, knit to end, picking up wraps and working them together with the sts they wrap. Place rem 16 (19, 20, 22, 23, 25) sts for left shoulder on holder.
Short-Row 8: Purl, picking up wraps and working them together with the sts they wrap. Place rem 16 (19, 20, 22, 23, 25) sts for right shoulder on holder.

FRONT

With CC and longer circ needle, CO 100 (111, 123, 137, 152, 163) sts using an elastic CO method.

Row 1 (RS): K36 (36, 38, 40, 42, 44), pm, p28 (39, 47, 57, 68, 75), pm, k36 (36, 38, 40, 42, 44).

Row 2 (WS): P36 (36, 38, 40, 42, 44), sm, k28 (39, 47, 57, 68, 75), sm, p36 (36, 38, 40, 42, 44).

Rep Rows 1 and 2 once more and remove markers on last row.

Change to MC. Work even in St st until piece meas 5½ (5½, 6, 6, 6½, 6½)" [14 (14, 15, 15, 16.5, 16.5) cm] from beg, ending with a WS row.

Waist Shaping:

Work same as Back until piece meas 11 (11½, 11½, 11½, 11½, 11½)" [28 (29, 29, 29, 29, 29) cm] from beg, ending with a WS row. 78 (87, 103, 119, 138, 151) sts rem on needle.

Next (inc) Row (RS): K26 (28, 28, 32, 34, 36), sm, M1R, knit to marker, M1L, sm, knit to end—2 sts increased.

Rep inc row every 4th row 10 (11, 11, 11, 7, 7) more times, then every RS row 0 (0, 0, 0, 5, 5) times. 100 (111, 127, 143, 164, 177) sts rem on needle.

Work even until piece meas 18 (18, 17½, 17½, 17, 17)" [45.5 (45.5, 44.5, 44.5, 43, 43) cm] from beg, ending with a WS row.

Shape Neck and Armholes

Mark center 2 (3, 3, 3, 2, 3) sts.

Next row (RS): BO 4 (4, 4, 6, 7, 7) sts, knit to marked sts, join a second ball of yarn and BO marked sts, then knit to end.

Next row (WS): BO 4 (4, 4, 6, 7, 7) sts, purl to end. 45 (50, 58, 64, 74, 80) sts rem for each side of front.

Working neck and armhole shaping at the same time, dec at beg of RS rows by working k2, ssk, and end of RS rows by working to last 4 sts, k2tog, k2. Dec 1 st at each armhole edge every RS row 2 (6, 10, 12, 15, 17) times, then every 4th row 5 (3, 3, 3, 5, 5) times. AT THE SAME TIME, dec 1 st at each neck edge every 4th row 6 (8, 7, 7, 5, 5) times, then every RS row 16 (14, 18, 20, 26, 28) times. [16 (19, 20, 22, 23, 25) sts rem when all dec is complete] AT THE SAME TIME, when armhole measures 7 (7½, 8, 8½, 9, 9½)" [18 (19, 20.5, 21.5, 23, 24) cm], shape shoulders same as for Back beg on next RS row.

Place shoulder sts on dpns and join shoulders using 3-Needle Bind-Off, holding RS together.

Lay Front and Back on table or other flat surface, with WS tog and side and bottom edges even, and pockets extending out to the sides.

Sew side seams, making sure Front is sewn to Back and keeping Pockets free. Fold Pockets to Front so Rev St st edging matches up along lower edge of Front. Sew front edges of Pockets to front, and CO edges together.

SLEEVES (MAKE 2)

With shorter circ needle, using MC, and with RS facing, and with RS facing, beg at center of underarm BO, pick up and k40 (44, 49, 54, 56, 59) sts along one side of armhole, 1 st in shoulder seam (pm to mark this st), then 40 (44, 49, 54, 56, 59) along rem side of armhole to center of underarm BO (approx 2 sts for every 3 rows).

Shape Sleeve Cap

Short-Row 1 (RS): Knit to 14 (15, 17, 18, 19, 20) sts past shoulder marker, w&t.

Short-Row 2 (WS): Purl to 14 (15, 17, 18, 19, 20) sts past shoulder marker, w&t.

Short-row 3: Knit to wrapped st on other side of shoulder marker, knit wrapped st, picking up wrap and working it together with the st it wraps, k1, w&t.

Short-row 4: Purl to wrapped st on other side of shoulder marker, purl wrapped st, picking up wrap and working it together with the st it wraps, p1, w&t.

Rep Short-Rows 3 and 4 until 13 (14, 16, 18, 18, 19) sts rem unworked at each end. Work 2 rows of St st over all sts picking up rem wraps and working them together with the sts they wrap. With RS facing, pm for beg of rnd.

Cont in St st in the rnd for 1½" [4 cm]. Change to dpns when needed.

Shape Underarm

Next (dec) rnd: K1, k2tog, knit to last 3 sts, ssk, k1—2 sts decreased.

Rep dec rnd every 4th rnd once more, then every other rnd 6 (6, 5, 5, 4, 4) times. 67 (75, 87, 97, 103, 109) sts rem on needle.

Cont even in St st until sleeve meas 8¼ (8½, 8½, 8¾, 8¾, 9)" [21 (21.5, 21.5, 22, 22, 23) cm] from armhole, or approx elbow-length.

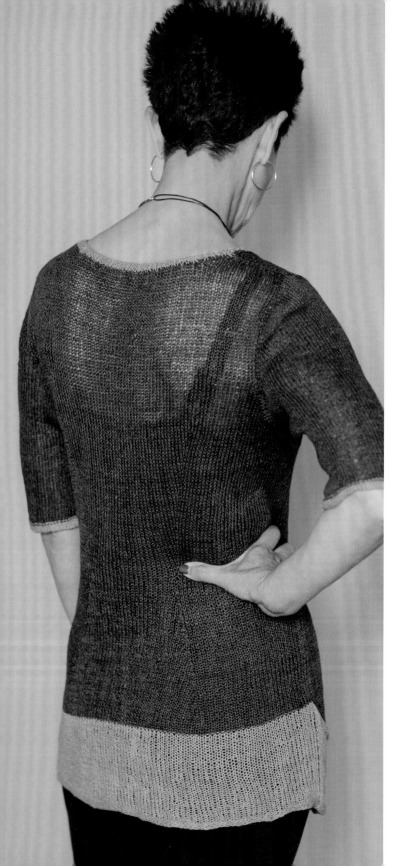

Change to CC. Purl 4 rnds. BO all sts purlwise.

NECK BAND

With longer circ needle, using CC, and RS facing, beg at bottom of front neck, pick up and k35 (36, 37, 38, 39, 40) sts along right edge to shoulder, 40 (41, 47, 51, 58, 63) sts along back neck, then 35 (36, 37, 38, 39, 40) along left edge to bottom of front neck. 110 (113, 121, 127, 136, 143) sts. Work back and forth in Rev St st for 3 rows. BO all sts purlwise.
Sew ends of neckband to neck edge at bottom of front neck with right side overlapping top of left side.

FINISHING

Weave in all loose ends; since the pieces will be somewhat sheer, work carefully so ends won't poke out or create bulk. Wet-block sweater, gently patting into place on blocking board, using schematic measurements as a guide. Pin if necessary, being careful not to stretch too much.

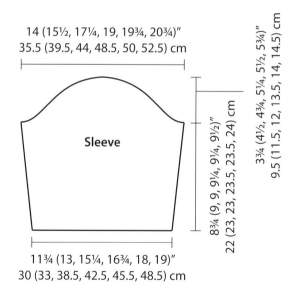

14 (15½, 17¼, 19, 19¾, 20¾)"
35.5 (39.5, 44, 48.5, 50, 52.5) cm

Sleeve

3¾ (4½, 4¾, 5¼, 5½, 5¾)"
9.5 (11.5, 12, 13.5, 14, 14.5) cm

8¾ (9, 9, 9¼, 9¼, 9½)"
22 (23, 23, 23.5, 23.5, 24) cm

11¾ (13, 15¼, 16¾, 18, 19)"
30 (33, 38.5, 42.5, 45.5, 48.5) cm

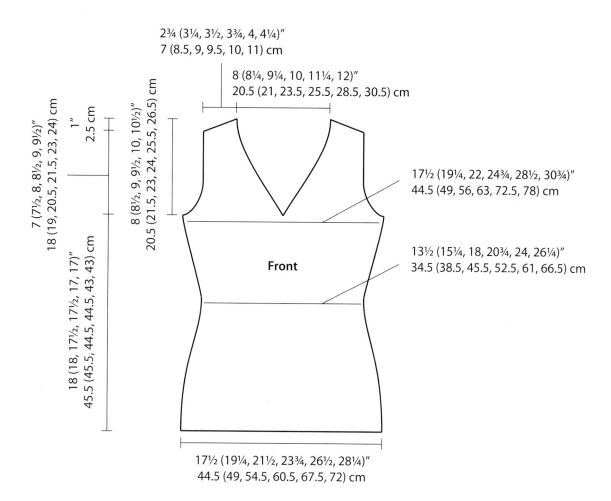

2¾ (3¼, 3½, 3¾, 4, 4¼)"
7 (8.5, 9, 9.5, 10, 11) cm

8 (8¼, 9¼, 10, 11¼, 12)"
20.5 (21, 23.5, 25.5, 28.5, 30.5) cm

7 (7½, 8, 8½, 9, 9½)"
18 (19, 20.5, 21.5, 23, 24) cm

1"
2.5 cm

8 (8½, 9, 9½, 10, 10½)"
20.5 (21.5, 23, 24, 25.5, 26.5) cm

18 (18, 17½, 17½, 17, 17)"
45.5 (45.5, 44.5, 44.5, 43, 43) cm

17½ (19¼, 22, 24¾, 28½, 30¾)"
44.5 (49, 56, 63, 72.5, 78) cm

13½ (15¼, 18, 20¾, 24, 26¼)"
34.5 (38.5, 45.5, 52.5, 61, 66.5) cm

Front

17½ (19¼, 21½, 23¾, 26½, 28¼)"
44.5 (49, 54.5, 60.5, 67.5, 72) cm

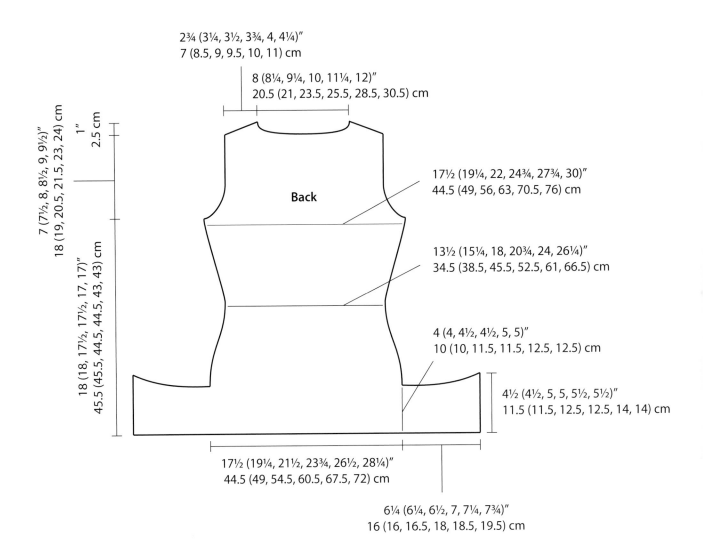

2¾ (3¼, 3½, 3¾, 4, 4¼)"
7 (8.5, 9, 9.5, 10, 11) cm

8 (8¼, 9¼, 10, 11¼, 12)"
20.5 (21, 23.5, 25.5, 28.5, 30.5) cm

Back

17½ (19¼, 22, 24¾, 27¾, 30)"
44.5 (49, 56, 63, 70.5, 76) cm

13½ (15¼, 18, 20¾, 24, 26¼)"
34.5 (38.5, 45.5, 52.5, 61, 66.5) cm

4 (4, 4½, 4½, 5, 5)"
10 (10, 11.5, 11.5, 12.5, 12.5) cm

4½ (4½, 5, 5, 5½, 5½)"
11.5 (11.5, 12.5, 12.5, 14, 14) cm

7 (7½, 8, 8½, 9, 9½)"
18 (19, 20.5, 21.5, 23, 24) cm

1"
2.5 cm

18 (18, 17½, 17½, 17, 17)"
45.5 (45.5, 44.5, 44.5, 43, 43) cm

17½ (19¼, 21½, 23¾, 26½, 28¼)"
44.5 (49, 54.5, 60.5, 67.5, 72) cm

6¼ (6¼, 6½, 7, 7¼, 7¾)"
16 (16, 16.5, 18, 18.5, 19.5) cm

SAIL AWAY

Very few wool blend fibers are featured in KNITS THAT BREATHE for the obvious reason: wool is too warm to wear during a personal summer, and itchy to those with sensitive skin. But in addition to wool, Lorna's Laces *Sportmate* includes Outlast®, a patented fiber that absorbs, stores, and releases body heat, adapting automatically to keep the wearer comfortable. One artful fold and two short seams turn a simple length of all-over lace into a breezy shrug that is completed with gathered cuffs.

SIZES

S (M, L, XL, XXL, XXXL)
Finished width of rectangle (end to end) = 45¾ (48, 50¼, 52¼, 54¾, 56¾)" [116 (122, 127.5, 132.5) cm]
Finished length of rectangle (top to bottom) = 18½ (20½, 22½, 24½, 26, 27½)" [47 (52, 57, 62, 66, 70) cm]

MATERIALS

Lorna's Laces Sportmate [270 yds (247 m)/3.5 oz (100 g), 70% Superwash Merino Wool, 30% Outlast® Viscose]. Color: Cermak #512. 3 (4, 4, 5, 6, 6) skeins.
One US 5 (3.75 mm) 29" (74 cm) to 32" (80 cm) circular needles, or size needed to obtain correct gauge.
One US 4 (3.5 mm) 12" (30 cm) to 16" (40 cm) circular needle and set of 4 or 5 double-pointed needles.
Tapestry needle
Stitch markers
US F-5 (3.75 mm) crochet hook

GAUGE

22 sts and 32 rows = 4" (10 cm) in lace pattern using larger needles, blocked.

PATTERN NOTES

This shrug is worked back and forth in rows from the bottom up. A circular needle is used to accommodate the large number of stitches. Once the main part of the shrug has been blocked and assembled, cuff stitches are worked in the round down from the ends, with options given for either gathered cuffs or loose kimono sleeve edging. Body edging is worked in Single Crochet. Lace patt instructions are provided in both written row-by-row and chart formats.

Lace Pattern
(multiple of 6 sts + 2)
Row 1 (RS): K1, *k4, k2tog, yo; rep from * to last st, k1.
Row 2: P1, *yo, p1, p2tog, p3; rep from * to last st, p1.
Row 3: K1, *k2, k2tog, k2, yo; rep from * to last st, k1.
Row 4: P1, *yo, p3, p2tog, p1; rep from * to last st, p1.
Row 5: K1, *k2tog, k4, yo; rep from * to last st, k1.
Row 6: P2, *p4, yo, p2tog; rep from * to end.
Row 7: K1, *k1, yo, k3, k2tog; rep from * to last st, k1.
Row 8: P1, *p2tog, p2, yo, p2; rep from * to last st, p1.
Row 9: K1, *k3, yo, k1, k2tog; rep from * to last st, k1.
Row 10: P1, *p2tog, yo, p4; rep from * to last st, p1.
Rep Rows 1 – 10.

DIRECTIONS

With larger circ needle, use Cable method to CO 236 (248, 260, 272, 284, 296) sts. Knit 6 rows.

Lace Set-Up
Next (set-up) row (RS): K3, pm, work Row 1 of Lace patt to last 3 sts, pm, k3.

BODY
Working first and last 3 sts of every row in garter st, cont Lace patt over rem sts until piece meas approximately 17¾ (19¾, 21¾, 23¾, 25¼, 26¾)" [45 (50, 55, 60.5, 64, 68) cm]. Knit 6 rows. BO all sts knitwise.
Block piece to finished measurements. Fold piece in half lengthwise. Sew 10 (10½, 11, 11, 11¼, 11½)" [25.5 (26.5, 28, 28) cm] together from each edge toward the center, leaving 23 (24, 25¼, 27½, 29¼, 30¾)" [58 (61, 64, 70, 74.5, 78) cm] open at center.

GATHERED CUFFS, OPTION #1 (MAKE 2)
With smaller circ needle or dpns and RS facing, pick up and knit 57 (60, 63, 69, 73, 79) sts around sleeve opening. Pm for beg of rnd, and join to work in the rnd.

Next (dec) rnd: [K3, k2tog] 11 (12, 12, 13, 14, 15) times, k2 (0, 3, 4, 3, 4). 46 (48, 51, 56, 59, 64) sts rem.
Rnd 1: Knit.
Rnd 2: Purl.
Rep last 2 rnds 8 (8, 11, 11) more times. Knit 1 more row. BO all sts purlwise.

KIMONO SLEEVES, OPTION #2 (MAKE 2)

With larger needle and RS facing, pick up and knit 150 (160, 170, 180) sts around sleeve opening, or approx 3 of every 4 sts. Pm for beg of rnd, and join.
Rnd 1: Knit.
Rnd 2: Purl.
Rep Rnds 1 and 2, 8 more times. Knit 1 more rnd. BO all sts purl-wise. With crochet hook and RS facing, work 1 rnd of single crochet around sleeve opening, join with a slip st in the first st. Fasten off.

BODY EDGING

With crochet hook and RS facing, begin at center of back neck and work 1 rnd of single crochet around opening, working 1 st in every 3 of 4 sts around, and then join with a slip st in the first st. Fasten off.

FINISHING

Weave in ends.
Fold shrug in half lengthwise, lining up cuffs and body edging. Pin cuffs and edging flat. Mist them with water and allow to dry. This will relax cuffs and edging slightly so they are smooth.

CHART KEY

☐ k on RS, p on WS

⊙ yo

⧄ k2tog on RS, p2tog on WS

☐ repeat

LACE PATTERN

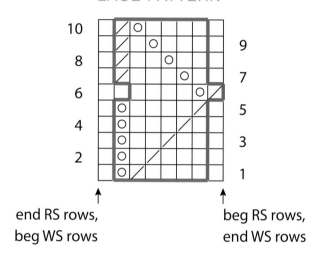

end RS rows, beg WS rows

beg RS rows, end WS rows

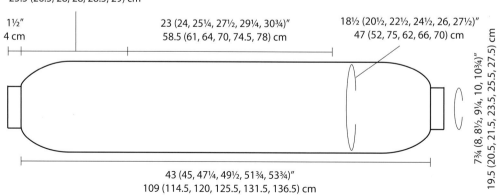

10 (10½, 11, 11, 11¼, 11½)"
25.5 (26.5, 28, 28, 28.5, 29) cm

1½"
4 cm

23 (24, 25¼, 27½, 29¼, 30¾)"
58.5 (61, 64, 70, 74.5, 78) cm

18½ (20½, 22½, 24½, 26, 27½)"
47 (52, 75, 62, 66, 70) cm

7¾ (8, 8½, 9¼, 10, 10¾)"
19.5 (20.5, 21.5, 23.5, 25.5, 27.5) cm

43 (45, 47¼, 49½, 51¾, 53¾)"
109 (114.5, 120, 125.5, 131.5, 136.5) cm

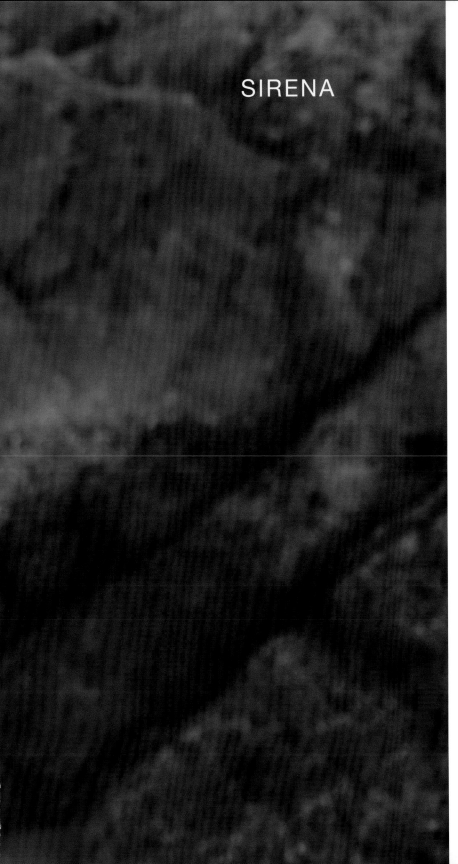

SIRENA

Sometimes you need a dressed-up evening top that still feels effortless. And what could be more alluring than a breezy silk and linen top that features open shoulders, feminine lace, and subtle beading? Although its sophisticated appearance would suggest otherwise, minimal shaping and easy lace pair with ridiculously short seams to make it a surprisingly quick knit. Some may decide that the discreet shimmer of beads at the lace hem is gilding the lily, and should feel free to omit them. Worn with a long skirt or silk pants over a slinky camisole, Sirena will earn its place at the front of your closet.

SIZES

XS (S, M, L, XL, XXL) To be worn with 2-3" positive ease.
Finished width at bust = 36¼ (40¼, 44¼, 49¾, 53¾, 57¾)" [92 (102, 112.5, 126.5, 136.5, 146.5)].
Length = 24 (24 1/2, 24 1/2, 27, 27 1/2, 28)" [61 (62, 62, 68.5, 70, 71) cm]

MATERIALS

Hand Maiden Fine Yarn Flaxen [273 yds (250 m)/3.5oz (100 g), 65% silk, 35% linen]. Color: Periwinkle. 4 (5, 5, 6, 6, 7) skeins.
One US 6 (4 mm) 29" (74 cm) circular needle, or size needed to obtain correct gauge.
Size 8/0 (2.5 mm) approx 226 (272, 298, 324, 350, 376) glass beads
Size US 14 (0.50 mm) steel crochet hook (for placing beads)
Size G-6 (4 mm) crochet hook (for neck edging)
Stitch markers
Tapestry needle
One ⅝" [16 mm] button
Waste yarn

GAUGE

24 sts and 27 rows = 4" (10 cm) in Faggoting Pattern, blocked

PATTERN NOTES

Sirena's lace hem is worked in two separate pieces to allow for side slits. Both halves are then joined to work in the round to the armholes. The work is separated to cast on stitches for the sleeves. The top's front and back are worked back and forth in two separate pieces up to the shoulders. The only seams are the underside of the sleeves and the shoulder/sleeve edges.

STITCH GUIDE

Lace pattern directions are provided in both written row-by-row and chart formats.

Beaded Lace Hem
(multiple of 12 sts + 1)

Row 1 (RS): *K1, yo, k4, s2kp, k4, yo; rep from * to last st, k1.
Row 2 and all other WS rows: Purl.
Row 3: *Place bead, k1, yo, k3, s2kp, k3, yo, k1; rep from * to last st, place bead.
Row 5: *K1, yo, ssk, yo, k2, s2kp, k2, yo, k2tog, yo; rep from * to last st, k1.
Row 7: *Place bead, k1, yo, ssk, yo, k1, s2kp, k1, yo, k2tog, yo, k1; rep from * to last st, place bead.
Row 9: *Place bead, k2, yo, ssk, yo, s2kp, yo, k2tog, yo, k2; rep from * to last st, place bead.
Row 11: *K1, place bead, k2, yo, ssk, place bead, k2tog, yo, k2, place bead; rep from * to last st, k1.
Row 13: *Place bead, k1, place bead, k2, yo, s2kp, yo, k2, place bead, k1; rep from * to last st, place bead.
Row 15: *K1, place bead, k3, yo, s2kp, yo, k3, place bead; rep from * to last st, k1.
Rows 17 and 19: Place bead, k4, yo, s2kp, yo, k4; rep from * to last st, place bead.
Row 20: Purl.

Faggoting (worked back and forth)
(multiple of 12 sts + 1)

Row 1 (RS): *K5, yo, s2kp, yo, k4; rep from * to last st, k1.
Row 2 (WS): Purl.
Rep these 2 rows.

Faggoting (worked in the round)
(multiple of 12 sts)

Rnd 1: *K5, yo, s2kp, yo, k4; rep from * around.
Rnd 2: Knit.
Rep these 2 rows.

Place Bead (Optional): I prefer the crochet hook method for adding beads to the lace hem. To place a bead using this method, place a bead on the smaller crochet hook, and insert the hook into the stitch where you want to add the bead. Lift the stitch off the left needle, and slide the bead onto the stitch. Place the stitch back on the left needle, and knit the stitch. You can also check out Lily Chin's great description of this technique in *Knit and Crochet with Beads*, on pp. 48-9. She calls her method "Hoisted atop Stitches," but by any name it is a simple and relatively quick way to add a small number of beads to a knitted project without the need for tedious pre-stringing.

DIRECTIONS

BORDER (MAKE 2)
CO 121 (133, 145, 157, 169, 181) sts.

Row 1 (RS): K6, pm, work Row 1 of Lace Border patt to last 6 sts, pm, k6.
Row 2 (WS): K6, sm, purl to last 6 sts, sm, k6.
Cont as est through Row 20 of Beaded Lace Hem patt.
Next row (RS): K6, sm, work Row 1 of Faggoting to last 6 sts, sm, k6.
Next row: K6, sm, purl to last 6 sts, sm, k6.
Rep last 2 rows 3 (3, 4, 4, 5, 5) more times.
Place sts onto waste yarn and make second Border.

BODY
With RS facing, place sts for both borders on circ needle and pm between pieces to mark beg of rnd and side of body. [242 (266, 290, 314, 338, 362) sts. Join to work in the rnd.

Next (set-up) rnd: *K6, work Rnd 1 of Faggoting patt to 6 sts before side marker, k6; rep from * once more.

Next rnd: *K6, work Rnd 2 of Faggoting to 6 sts before side marker, k6; rep from * once more.

Cont as est until piece meas 6 (6½, 6½, 7, 7, 7½)" [15 (16.5, 16.5, 18, 18, 19) cm] from bottom edge.

Shape Waist
Next (dec) rnd: *K1, ssk, work to 3 sts before side marker, k2tog, k1; rep from * once more. 2 sts decreased

Rep dec rnd every 12th rnd 3 times, then every 10th rnd 2 (2, 2, 3, 3, 3) times. 218 (242, 266, 286, 310, 334) sts.

Sizes L (XL, XXL) only
Next (inc) rnd: *K1, M1, work to 1 st before side marker, M1, k1; rep from * once more. 4 sts increased

Rep inc rnd every 4th rnd twice more. 298 (322, 346) sts

All sizes
Work even until piece meas 16 (16, 16, 18, 18, 18)," [43 (47, 48.5, 48.5, 49.5, 51) cm] from bottom edge.

FRONT AND SLEEVES:
Divide work at markers and place last 109 (121, 133, 149, 161, 173) sts on waste yarn. 109 (121, 133, 149, 161, 173) sts rem for front

Next row (RS): Using Knitted method, CO 25 (25, 25, 35, 35, 35) sts for Left Sleeve, work to end of row. 134 (146, 158, 184, 196, 208) sts

Next row (WS): Using Knitted method, CO 26 (26, 26, 38, 38, 38) sts for Right Sleeve. purl to end of row. 159 (171, 183, 219, 231, 243) sts

Next row (RS): K6, *yo, s2kp, yo, k9; rep from * to last 9 sts, yo, s2kp, yo, k6.

Next row (WS): K6, purl to last 6 sts, k6.

Cont as est until sleeve meas 5 (5½, 5½, 6, 6½, 7)" [12.5, 14, 14, 15, 16.5, 18) cm], ending with a WS row.

Shape Front Neck
Mark center 33 (33, 33, 39, 39, 39) sts.

Next row (RS): Work as est to marker, join second ball of yarn, BO marked sts, work to end. [63 (69, 75, 90, 96, 102) sts rem each side]

Work both sides at the same time, BO 3 sts every other row at neck edge 1 (1, 1, 2, 2, 2) time(s), then 2 sts 1 (2, 2, 1, 1, 1) time(s). Dec 1 st at neck edge every RS row 0 (1, 1, 2, 2, 3) time(s). 58 (61, 67, 80, 86, 91) sts

Work even until sleeve meas 8 (8½, 8½, 9, 9½, 10)" 20.5 (21.5, 21.5, 23, 24, 25.5) cm]. BO rem sts.

BACK AND SLEEVES
Work Back same as Front until sleeve meas 5 (5½, 4½, 5, 5½, 5½)" [12.5 (14, 11.5, 12.5, 14, 14) cm], ending with a WS row.

Back Split
Next row (RS): Work 78 (84, 90, 108, 114, 120), k2tog, join a second ball of yarn and work to end. 79 (85, 91, 109, 115, 121 sts each side

Next row (WS): Work as est to 4 (4, 4, 6, 6, 6) sts before split, k4 (4, 4, 6, 6, 6); k4 (4, 4, 6, 6, 6), work as est to end.

Work even until sleeve meas 8 (8½, 8½, 9, 9½, 10)" 20.5 (21.5, 21.5, 23, 24, 25.5) cm]. BO rem sts.

FINISHING
Wet block garment, pinning lace points at the hem and opening up the faggoting. Weave in all ends. Sew underarm seams.

Try on garment, and use pins to mark desired width of shoulder seam (2 – 3" [5 – 7.5 cm] should be sufficient for optimal bra strap concealment). Sew shoulder seams and garter bands at cuff edge, leaving top of sleeves open.

Neck edging
With larger crochet hook and WS facing, beg at neck split and work 1 row of Single Crochet along neck edge, chain 6 to 8, then sl st in second row down from neck edge for button loop, adjusting length of loop as needed. Sew button to right edge of split opposite button loop.

CHART KEY

☐	k on RS, p on WS
⊡	yo
⊿	k2tog
◺	ssk
⬘	s2kp
B	place bead (see Pattern Notes)
☐	repeat

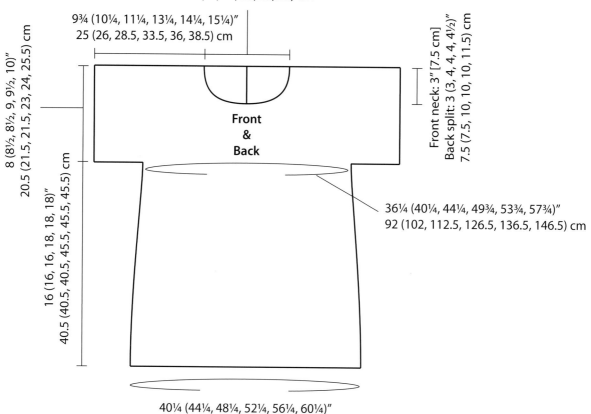

7¼ (8¼, 8¼, 9¾, 9¾, 10¼)"
18.5 (21, 21, 25, 25, 26) cm

9¾ (10¼, 11¼, 13¼, 14¼, 15¼)"
25 (26, 28.5, 33.5, 36, 38.5) cm

Front neck: 3" [7.5 cm]
Back split: 3 (3, 4, 4, 4, 4½)"
7.5 (7.5, 10, 10, 10, 11.5) cm

**Front
&
Back**

8 (8½, 8½, 9, 9½, 10)"
20.5 (21.5, 21.5, 23, 24, 25.5) cm

36¼ (40¼, 44¼, 49¾, 53¾, 57¾)"
92 (102, 112.5, 126.5, 136.5, 146.5) cm

16 (16, 16, 18, 18, 18)"
40.5 (40.5, 40.5, 45.5, 45.5, 45.5) cm

40¼ (44¼, 48¼, 52¼, 56¼, 60¼)"
102 (112.5, 122.5, 132.5, 143, 153) cm

BEADED LACE HEM

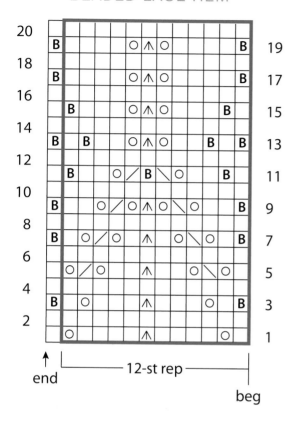

20
B | | | | ○ ∧ ○ | | | | B   19
18
B | | | | ○ ∧ ○ | | | | B   17
16
| B | | | ○ ∧ ○ | | | B | 15
14
B | B | | ○ ∧ ○ | | B | B   13
12
| B | | ○ / B \ ○ | | B | 11
10
B | | ○ | / ○ ∧ ○ \ | ○ | B   9
8
B | | ○ / ○ | ∧ | ○ \ ○ | B   7
6
| ○ / ○ | | ∧ | | ○ \ ○ | 5
4
B | ○ | | | ∧ | | | ○ | B   3
2
| ○ | | | | ∧ | | | | ○ | 1

↑
end

├── 12-st rep ──┤

beg

FAGGOTING

2
| | | | | ○ ∧ ○ | | | | | 1

↑
end

├── 12-st rep ──┤

beg

SORBET

Even the hottest among us occasionally finds herself in an overly air conditioned office, a drafty theater, or out and about on an unexpectedly cool evening. In these situations, a little bit of wool can be a godsend, especially when it's combined with temperature-regulating fibers such as silk and seaweed. This shrug is an ideal project for the luxury yarn languishing in a knitter's stash because it requires just a few skeins. A light worsted weight 50/50 merino and silk blend would substitute nicely and have a similar feel. Feel free to work the sleeves to the wrist; the lace cuff will be equally fetching there. Those who think a shrug or short cardigan is best suited only to the young and the skinny should give this one a try over a long tank or tunic – the proportions will be surprisingly right!

SIZES

XS (S, M, L, XL, XXL)

Finished width at bust = 32¾ (35¾, 40, 44, 48¼, 51½)" [83 (91, 101.5, 112, 122.5, 131) cm]

Finished length, from back neck = 15 1/4 (16 1/4, 17 3/4, 18 1/2, 19 3/4, 20 1/4)" [38.5 (41, 45, 47, 50, 51.5) cm]

MATERIALS

Blue Moon Fiber Arts Marine-Silk Worsted (243 yds (222 m)/3.5 oz (100 g), 51% silk, 29% Merino, 20% Sea Cell ® Rayon). Color: Buttah. 3 (3, 4, 4, 4, 4) skeins.

One US 5 (3.75 mm) 16" (40 cm) circular needle

One US 6 (4 mm) 29" (74 cm) to 40" (100 cm) circular needle and set of 4 or 5 double-pointed or 16" (40 cm) circular needle, or size needed to obtain correct gauge.

Stitch markers in at least 2 different colors

Tapestry needle

Scrap yarn or stitch holders

One 1/2" (13 mm) decorative button

GAUGE

23 sts and 26 rows = 4" (10 cm) in St st using larger needles, blocked.

PATTERN NOTES

This raglan shoulder, elbow-length sleeved shrug is worked back and forth from the top down (except for the sleeves, which are worked in the round). The body and sleeves are worked in stockinette stitch except where noted. Always slip sts purlwise with the yarn in back.

A circular needle is used to accommodate the large number of body sts; change to the longer needle when necessary. Do not join when working the body. Both written row-by-row and charted directions are provided for the Feather Lace panels that run along the front of the shrug and the cuffs.

STITCH GUIDE

Feather Lace (Multiple of 12 sts plus 1)
Row 1 and all other WS rows: Purl.
Row 2 (RS): K1, *yo, ssk, k7, k2tog, yo, k1; rep from * to end.
Row 4: K1, *yo, k1, ssk, k5, k2tog, k1, yo, k1; rep from * to end.
Row 6: K1, *yo, k2, ssk, k3, k2tog, k2, yo, k1; rep from *.
Row 8: K1, *yo, k3, ssk, k1, k2tog, k3, yo, k1; rep from *.
Row 10: K1, *yo, k4, ssk2p, k4, yo, k1; rep from *.
Rep rows 1 – 10 for pattern.

DIRECTIONS
BODY
With smaller 16" (40 cm) circ needle, CO 70 (80, 84, 88, 104, 108) sts. Do not join. Rows begin at Center Front.
Row 1 (RS): Sl 3 purlwise wyib, purl to last 3 sts, sl 3.
Row 2 (WS): P3, knit to last 3 sts, p3.
Rows 3 & 5: Rep Row 1.
Row 4 (Buttonhole - WS): P3, yo, k2tog, knit to last 3 sts, p3.
Row 6 (Set-up Row – WS): P3, pm for front edge, p14 for Right Front, pm, p1 for raglan inc, pm, p4 (6, 6, 6, 10, 10) for Right Sleeve, pm, p1 for raglan inc, pm, p24 (30, 34, 38, 46, 50) for Back, pm, p1 for raglan inc, pm, p4 (6, 6, 6, 10 10) for Left Sleeve, pm, p1 for raglan inc, pm, p14 for Left Front, pm, p3 for front edge.
Change to larger circ needle, changing to longer circ needle as necessary to accommodate the increasing number of sts.

Begin yoke shaping and Feather Lace front panels

Next row (RS): Sl 3 wyib, sm, work Row 2 of Feather Lace across next 13 sts, k1, *yo, sm, k1, sm, yo, knit to next marker: rep from * twice more, yo, sm, k1, sm, yo, k1, work Row 2 of Feather Lace across next 13 sts, sm, sl 3. 8 sts increased.

Next row: Purl, slipping markers as you come to them. Cont inc every RS row 28 (30, 34, 39, 41, 43) more times, then every 4th row 1 (1, 1, 0, 0, 0) time.

AT THE SAME TIME, when 8 (4, 2, 2, 0, 0) rows have been worked after the WS Set-Up row, shape the neck every RS row 1 (1, 1, 1, 2, 3) time(s) as follows: P3, m1, cont in est patt to last 3 sts, m1, p3.

When all raglan and neck increases have been completed, there will be 312 (338, 374, 410, 416, 468) sts; 84 (94, 106, 118, 130, 138) sts for the back, 48 (50, 54, 58, 61, 64) sts for each front and 66 (72, 80, 88, 96, 100) sts for each sleeve, including the sts between markers for raglan increases.

Divide Body and Sleeves

Next row (RS): Removing markers as you come to them, work 48 (50, 54, 58, 61, 64) sts for Left Front, place the 66 (72, 80, 88, 96, 100) sts for Left Sleeve on waste yarn, CO 8 (10, 12, 14, 16, 18) sts and place new marker at the center of these CO sts to mark the left side "seam," k84 (94, 106, 118, 130, 138) sts for the Back, place the 66 (72, 80, 88, 96, 100) sts for Right Sleeve on a waste yarn, CO 8 (10, 12, 14, 16, 18) sts and place a new marker at the center of these CO sts to mark the right side "seam," then work across 48 (50, 54, 58, 61, 64) sts for the Right Front. 196 (214, 238, 262, 286, 304) sts; 52 (55, 60, 65, 69, 73) sts for each front and 92 (104, 118, 132, 146, 156) sts for the back.

Lower Body

Next row (WS): Purl.

Next row (RS): Sl 3 purlwise wyib, work next 14 sts in est patt, knit to 1 st before marker, sl 1 purlwise wyib, knit to next marker, sl 1 purlwise wyib, knit to last 17 sts, work next 14 sts in est patt, sl 3 purlwise wyib.

Cont even until piece meas 5 (5¼, 5½, 5½, 6, 6)" [12.5 (13.5, 14, 14, 15, 15) cm] from Dividing Row. Work 4 rows in Rev St st. BO all sts loosely.

SLEEVES: MAKE 2.

Place 66 (72, 80, 88, 96, 100) sleeve sts on larger 16" (40 cm) circ needle, or divide them evenly over 3 or 4 dpns. With RS facing, pick up and k8 (10, 12, 14, 16, 18) sts across CO sts at bottom of armhole and pm at the center st of these sts to mark the end of rnd as well as the faux underam "seam" st, knit sleeve sts, then knit to marker. 74 (82, 92, 102, 112, 118) sts.

Work 2 (4, 4, 4, 2, 4) rnds in St st, slipping the first st of every other every other every other rnd, and ending with a rnd that begins with a slip st.

Shape Underarm

Dec 1 st at each end of next rnd, then every 2nd rnd 11 (10, 10, 11, 12, 11) times, as foll: K1, ssk, knit to last 2 sts, k2tog. 50 (60, 70, 78, 86, 94) sts rem. Work even if necessary until sleeve meas 4 (4, 4, 4½, 4½, 4½)" [10 (10, 10, 11.5, 11.5, 11.5) cm] from pick-up rnd. BO all sts loosely.

FEATHER STITCH CUFF BANDS: MAKE 2.

With smaller 16" (40 cm) circ needle or 2 dpns, CO 19 sts.

Row 1 (RS): Sl 3 sts purlwise, k2, work Row 2 of Feather Lace, k2.

Row 2 (WS): Purl.

Cont back and forth, working Feather Lace until 7 (8, 8, 9, 9, 10) rep have been worked, or until cuff fits around lower edge of sleeve. BO all sts.

FINISHING

Block to finished measurements. Weave in all loose ends. Stitch ends of cuff bands. Stitch cuff bands to sleeves with WS of cuff facing RS of sleeve, so that the cuff band "folds" back like a French cuff making sure to position cuff end seam on underside of arm. Stitch decorative button to Front Panel opposite buttonhole.

CHART KEY

- ☐ k on RS, p on WS
- ☉ yo
- ☑ k2tog
- ☒ ssk
- ☒ sk2p
- ◻ repeat

FEATHER LACE

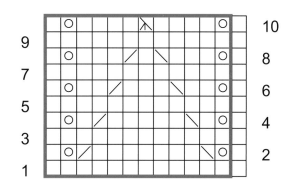

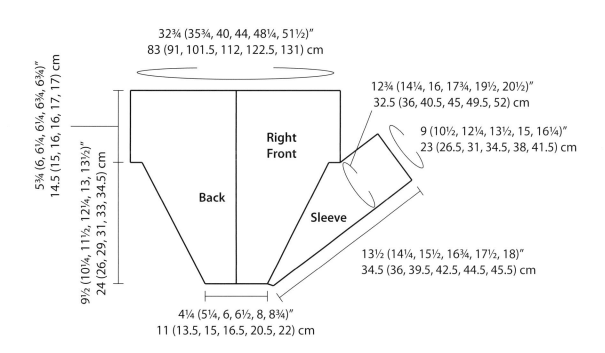

32¾ (35¾, 40, 44, 48¼, 51½)"
83 (91, 101.5, 112, 122.5, 131) cm

5¾ (6, 6¼, 6¼, 6¾, 6¾)"
14.5 (15, 16, 16, 17, 17) cm

12¾ (14¼, 16, 17¾, 19½, 20½)"
32.5 (36, 40.5, 45, 49.5, 52) cm

9 (10½, 12¼, 13½, 15, 16¼)"
23 (26.5, 31, 34.5, 38, 41.5) cm

Right Front

Back

Sleeve

9½ (10¼, 11½, 12¼, 13, 13½)"
24 (26, 29, 31, 33, 34.5) cm

13½ (14¼, 15½, 16¾, 17½, 18)"
34.5 (36, 39.5, 42.5, 44.5, 45.5) cm

4¼ (5¼, 6, 6½, 8, 8¾)"
11 (13.5, 15, 16.5, 20.5, 22) cm

SPLASH

This raglan-shouldered, lace front cardigan is worked back and forth from the top down. Pima cotton and bamboo fibers combine to create a soft and smooth, blissfully cool yarn that offers fantastic stitch definition, and results in a nearly seamless design that skims the body gracefully. Elbow-length sleeves are bordered in a single, slightly flared repeat of the front lace motif, and can be worked to ¾ or full length according to the preference of the wearer. Fasten Splash with a shawl pin or a favorite brooch, or let it cascade open.

SIZES

XS (S, M, L, XL, XXL)
Circumference at Bust, with fronts overlapping = 32½ (37, 40½, 44½, 50, 55½, 59½)" [82.5 (94, 103, 113, 127, 141, 151) cm]
Length = 24 (24 1/2, 26, 26, 27 3/4, 28 1/2)" [61 (62, 66, 66, 70.5, 72.5) cm]

MATERIALS

WEBS Valley Yarns Southwick [105 yds (96 m)/1.75oz (50 g), 52% pima cotton, 48% bamboo viscose. Color: Blue Lapis #04. 10 (11, 13, 14, 16, 17) skeins.
One US Size 6 (4 mm) 16" (40 cm) and 32" (80 cm) circular needle and set of 4 or 5 double-pointed needles, or size needed to obtain correct gauge.
One US Size 5 (3.5 mm) 16" (40 cm) circular needle
Stitch markers in two different colors
Tapestry needle
Waste yarn

GAUGE

21 sts and 23 rows = 4" (10 cm) in Lace Patt, blocked, on larger needles;
22 sts and 23 rows = 4" (10 cm) in St st, blocked, on larger needles.

PATTERN NOTES

There is no waist shaping in this cardigan and it is meant to be worn with positive ease. Faux side "seams" are created in the lower body on Right Side rows, by slipping one stitch with the yarn in back at each side marker. The cotton/bamboo fiber blend is stretchy but non-elastic, so it will "grow" with wear and should be stored folded and flat rather than on a hanger. Both written row-by-row and charted directions are included for the Lace pattern.

Lace Pattern (worked back and forth)
(multiple of 10 sts)
Rows 1, 3, and 5 (RS): *K1, ssk, k2, yo, k1, yo, k2, k2tog; rep from * to end.
Row 2 and all other WS rows: Purl.
Row 7: *K1, yo, ssk, k5, k2tog; rep from * to end.
Row 9: *K2, yo, ssk, k3, k2tog, yo, k1; rep from * to end.
Row 11: *K3, yo, ssk, k1, k2tog, yo, k2; rep from * to end.
Row 13: *K4, yo, s2kp, yo, k3; rep from * to end.
Row 14: Purl.
Rep these 14 rows.

Lace Pattern (worked in the round)
(multiple of 10 sts)
Rnds 1, 3, and 5 (RS): *K1, ssk, k2, yo, k1, yo, k2, k2tog; rep from * to end.
Rnd 2 and all other even-numbered rnds: Knit.
Rnd 7: *K1, yo, ssk, k5, k2tog; rep from * to end.
Rnd 9: *K2, yo, ssk, k3, k2tog, yo, k1; rep from * to end.
Rnd 11: *K3, yo, ssk, k1, k2tog, yo, k2; rep from * to end.
Rnd 13: *K4, yo, s2kp, yo, k3; rep from * to end.
Rnd 14: Purl.

DIRECTIONS

YOKE
Using either Long-Tail or the Cable Method, and larger long circ needle, CO 134 (160, 184, 208, 236, 262, 282) sts. Do not join.

Set-Up Row (WS): K44 (54, 64, 74, 84, 94, 104) for right front, pm, k2, pm, k4 for right sleeve, pm, k2, pm, k30 (36, 40, 44, 52, 58, 58) for back, pm, k2, pm, k4 for left sleeve, pm, k2, pm, k44 (54, 64, 74, 84, 94, 104) for left front.
Knit 4 more rows, slipping markers as you come to them.
Next Row (RS): K2, work Row 1 of Lace Patt over next 40 (50, 60, 70, 80, 90, 100) sts, k2, yo, sm, k2, sm, yo, k4, yo, sm, k2, sm, yo, knit to next marker, yo,

sm, k2, sm, yo, k4, yo, sm, k2, sm, yo, k2, work Row 1 of Lace Patt over next

40 (50, 60, 70, 80, 90, 100) sts, k2. [8 sts inc'd]

Next row (WS): K2, purl to last 2 sts, slipping markers as you come to them, k2.

Cont as est and inc every RS row 23 (24, 27, 31, 33, 37, 37) more times, then every 4th row 2 (2, 2, 0, 1, 2) time(s), working new sts in Lace Patt on each front as number of sts allow (make sure all yo "sts" can be worked with the accompanying dec), and in St st on Sleeves and Back, removing markers on last row. 342 (376, 424, 464, 516, 566, 602) sts; 71 (82, 95, 107, 120, 133, 145) sts for each front, 58 (60, 66, 70, 76, 82, 86) sts for each sleeve, and 84 (92, 102, 110, 124, 136, 142) sts for back, including sts between markers for raglans.

Divide body and sleeves

Next row (RS): Work 71 (82, 95, 107, 120, 133, 145) sts in est patt, place next 58 (60, 66, 70, 76, 82, 86) sts on waste yarn for sleeve, CO 3 (5, 5, 6, 7, 8, 11) sts, pm, CO 3 (5, 5, 6, 7, 8, 11) sts, k84 (92, 102, 110, 124, 136, 142) sts, place next 58 (60, 66, 70, 76, 82, 86) sts on waste yarn for sleeve, CO 3 (5, 5, 6, 7, 8) sts, pm, CO 3 (5, 5, 6, 7, 8, 11) sts, work to end as est. 238 (276, 312, 348, 392, 434, 474) sts

Lower Body

Next row (WS): K2, purl to last 2 sts, k2.

Next row (RS): K2, work next 70 (80, 90, 110, 120, 130, 150) sts in next row of Lace Patt, knit to 1 st before marker, sl 1 wyib, sm, knit to next marker, sm, sl 1 wyib, k1 (4, 7, 3, 4, 8, 3, work next 70 (80, 90, 110, 120, 130, 150) sts in next row of Lace Patt, k2.

Cont even in patt until lower body meas 13¾ (14, 14¼, 14¼, 14¾, 14¾, 15¼)" [35 (35.5, 36, 36, 37.5, 37.5, 38.5) cm] from dividing row, ending with a WS row.

Work 2 rows in Rev St st. BO all sts in Rev St st using an elastic BO.

SLEEVES: (MAKE 2)

Place held 58 (60, 66, 70, 76, 82, 86) sts from waste yarn to larger short circ needle or dpns, beg at center of underarm, pick up and k3 (5, 5, 6, 7, 8, 11) sts across CO sts,

knit to end, then pick up and k3 (5, 5, 6, 7, 8, 11) sts along rem edge of underarm. 64 (70, 76, 82, 90, 98, 108) sts. Pm for beg of rnd and join to work in the rnd.

Work even in St st for 1½" [4 cm].

Sizes XS (L) only

Knit 1 rnd and dec 4 (2) sts evenly spaced. 60 (80) sts rem

Sizes M (XXL, XXXL) only

Knit 1 rnd and inc 4 (2, 2) sts evenly spaced. 80 (100, 110) sts rem

All sizes

Work Lace Patt Rnds 1 – 14 once.

Purl 1 rnd. Knit 1 rnd. Purl 1 rnd. BO all sts knitwise.

FINISHING

Weave in loose ends.

Pin cardigan to blocking surface, folding fronts so that one side lies on top of the other and straightening side "seams." Spray with water and allow to dry.

CHART KEY

- ☐ k on RS, p on WS
- ☉ yo
- ⟋ k2tog
- ⟍ ssk
- ⋏ s2kp
- ☐ repeat

LACE PATTERN

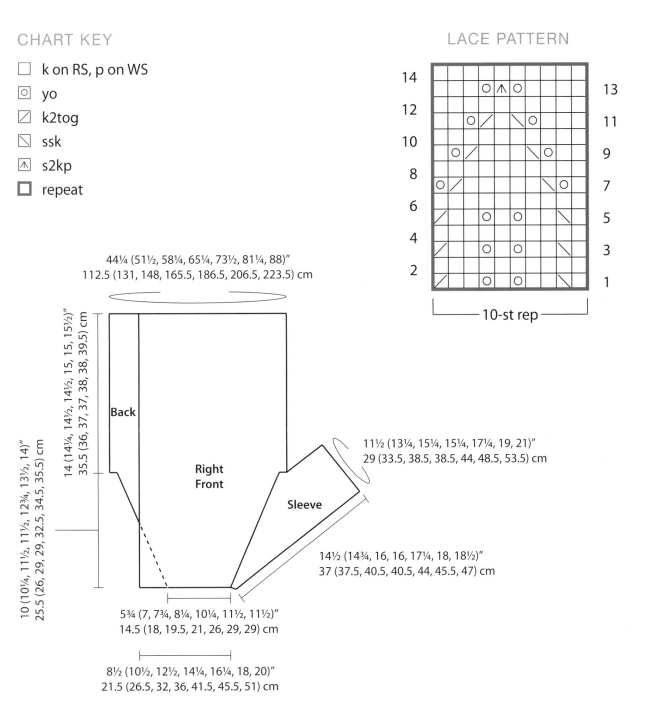

10-st rep

44¼ (51½, 58¼, 65¼, 73½, 81¼, 88)"
112.5 (131, 148, 165.5, 186.5, 206.5, 223.5) cm

14 (14¼, 14½, 14½, 15, 15, 15½)"
35.5 (36, 37, 37, 38, 38, 39.5) cm

Back

Right Front

Sleeve

10 (10¼, 11½, 11½, 12¾, 13½, 14)"
25.5 (26, 29, 29, 32.5, 34.5, 35.5) cm

11½ (13¼, 15¼, 15¼, 17¼, 19, 21)"
29 (33.5, 38.5, 38.5, 44, 48.5, 53.5) cm

14½ (14¾, 16, 16, 17¼, 18, 18½)"
37 (37.5, 40.5, 40.5, 44, 45.5, 47) cm

5¾ (7, 7¾, 8¼, 10¼, 11½, 11½)"
14.5 (18, 19.5, 21, 26, 29, 29) cm

8½ (10½, 12½, 14¼, 16¼, 18, 20)"
21.5 (26.5, 32, 36, 41.5, 45.5, 51) cm

STILL WATERS

A deep pool of clear cold water, dappled by sunlight and rippled by a soft breeze, is just one of the cooling visuals I imagine when my internal thermostat threatens a meltdown. As water slides over smooth stones, so the Still Waters Tee skims the body, its lacy side panels providing their own refreshing breeze. The 100% linen fiber wicks away moisture, drapes beautifully, and softens sublimely with wear. Alternative fiber blends such as sport weight cotton and linen, silk and linen, or bamboo and cotton would be good substitutes.

SIZES

XS (S, M, L, XL, XXL, XXXL, XXXXL)
Finished width at bust = 31 (35½, 40½, 43½, 47½, 51, 55, 59½)" [78.5 (90, 103, 110.5, 120.5, 129.5, 139.5, 151) cm]
Finished length, from back neck = 24 (24, 26, 26, 27, 27, 28, 29)" [61 (61, 66, 66, 68.5, 68.5, 71, 73.5) cm]

MATERIALS

Claudia Hand Painted Yarns Linen – Sport Weight [270 yds (247 m)/ approx. 3.5 oz (100 g), 100% linen]. Color: Blue Fields. 3 (3, 3, 4, 4, 4, 5, 5) skeins.
One US 6 (4 mm) 32" (80 cm) circular needle, or size needed to obtain correct gauge
Tapestry needle
Stitch markers
Stitch holders
Waste yarn
US E-4 (3.5 mm) crochet hook

GAUGE

23 sts and 26 rounds/rows = 4" (10 cm) in St st, blocked; 21 sts and 26 rounds/rows = 4" (10 cm) in Pebble Lace, blocked.

PATTERN NOTES

Tee is worked in one piece in the round from the bottom hem up to the armholes. From there, it is divided and worked back and forth in two separate pieces for the Front, Back, and short sleeves. The pieces are seamed at the shoulders and underarms to finish. There is no body shaping but the deep Pebble Lace border relaxes when blocked, resulting in a wider finished hip measurement. Lace instructions are provided in both written row-by-row and chart formats.

STITCH GUIDE

Pebble Lace: (Multiple of 4 sts plus 2, worked back and forth)
Row 1 (RS): K1, *yo, k1, yo, sk2p; rep from * to last st, k1.
Rows 2 and 4: Purl.
Row 3: K1, *sk2p, yo, k1, yo, rep from * to last st, k1.
Rep rows 1 – 4 for patt.

Pebble Lace: (Multiple of 4 sts plus 2, worked in the round)
Rnd 1: K1, *yo, k1, yo, sk2p; rep from * to last st, k1.
Rnds 2 and 4: Knit.
Rnd 3: K1, *sk2p, yo, k1, yo; rep from * to last st, k1.
Rep rnds 1 – 4 for patt.

DIRECTIONS

Pebble Lace Border Set-Up
CO 174 (198, 226, 242, 266, 286, 306, 334) sts using Cable method.
Row 1 (RS): Purl.
Row 2 (WS): Knit.
Rows 3 – 4: Rep Rows 1 and 2.
Row 5: Knit. Do not turn at end of row. Pm for beg of rnd and join to work in the rnd, taking care not to twist sts

Rnd 1 (set-up): K1, *yo, k1, yo, sk2p; rep from * to last st, yo, remove marker, slip last st to left needle, replace marker. 175 (199, 227, 243, 267, 287, 307, 334) sts.
Rnd 2: K2tog, knit to end of rnd. 174 (198, 226, 242, 266, 286, 306, 334) sts.
Cont from Rnd 3 of Pebble Lace patt, and work until piece meas approx 4 (4, 4, 5, 5, 5, 5½, 5½)" [10 (10, 10, 12.5, 12.5, 12.5, 14, 14) cm], ending with Rnd 4 of rep.

Next (set-up) rnd: Work Pebble Lace over first 26 (30, 38, 38, 42, 46, 50, 50) sts, pm, k61 (69, 75, 83, 91, 97, 103, 117) sts, pm, k1, yo, k2tog, yo, sk2p, [yo, k1, yo, sk2p] 5 (6, 8, 8, 9, 10, 11, 11) times, k1, pm, kfb, k57 (65, 71, 79, 87, 93, 99, 113), kfb. 174 (198, 226, 242, 266, 286, 306, 334) sts.

BODY

Next rnd: Knit.

Next rnd: *Work next row of Pebble Lace over next 26 (30, 38, 38, 42, 46, 50, 50) sts, sm, k61 (69, 75, 83, 91, 97, 103, 117), sm; rep from * once more.

Cont in est patt until piece meas approx 16½ (16, 17½, 17, 17, 17, 17½, 18)" [42 (40.5, 44.5, 43, 43, 43, 44.5, 45.5) cm] from CO, ending with Rnd 4 of rep. Break yarn.

Divide for Sleeves

Place first 13 (15, 19, 19, 21, 23, 25, 25) sts, and last 74 (84, 94, 102, 112, 120, 153, 167) sts on waste yarn for back. 87 (99, 113, 121, 133, 143, 153, 167) sts rem on needle for front, with 13 (15, 19, 19, 21, 23, 25, 25) sts in Pebble Lace patt on each end. Beg working back and forth.

FRONT

Row 1 (set-up, RS): Join new ball of yarn and CO 9 (11, 11, 15, 13, 15, 13, 13) sts using Cable method, work Row 1 of Pebble Lace over new sts and next 13 (15, 19, 19, 21, 23, 25, 25) sts, sm, k61 (69, 75, 83, 91, 97, 103, 117), sm, work Row 1 Pebble Lace over next 13 (13, 17, 17, 21, 21, 25, 25) sts, k0 (2, 2, 2, 0, 2, 0, 0), turn, CO 9 (11, 11, 15, 13, 15, 13, 13) sts using Cable method. 105 (121, 135, 151, 159, 173, 179, 193) sts.

Working 22 (26, 30, 34, 34, 38, 38, 38) sts at each end in Pebble Lace and center sts in St st, cont as est until Front meas 6½ (6¾, 7¼, 7½, 8½, 8½, 8½, 9)" [16.5 (17, 18.5, 19, 21.5, 21.5, 21.5, 23) cm] from underarm, ending with a WS row.

Shape Neck

Next row (RS): Work 35 (42, 47, 54, 57, 62, 63, 69) sts in est patt, join a second ball of yarn and BO center 35 (37, 41, 43, 45, 49, 53, 55) sts, cont in patt to end of row, Work each side of Front at the same time with separate balls of yarn.

Next row (WS): Purl.

Next (dec) row (RS): Work to 3 sts before neck edge, k2tog, k1; k1, ssk, work to end of row.

Rep last 2 rows 1 (2, 2, 3, 3, 3, 3, 4) more time(s). 33 (39, 44, 50, 53, 58, 59, 64) sts.

Place rem sts on holder.

BACK

Work Back same as the Front.

FINISHING

Return shoulder sts to needles. With RS tog, BO using 3-Needle BO.

With crochet hook and RS facing, work 1 row of single crochet around neck edge neck edge, working 3 out of every 4 sts.

Sew underarm seams. Weave in all loose ends.

Give tee a good soak in cool water, then wet-block to measurements on schematic.

CHART KEY

☐ k on RS, p on WS

⊡ yo

⧅ sk2p

☐ repeat

PEBBLE LACE

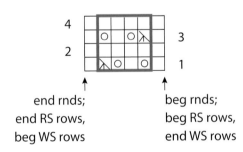

end rnds;   beg rnds;
end RS rows,   beg RS rows,
beg WS rows   end WS rows

Note: When working in the round, read all chart rows from right to left; when working back and forth, read RS rows from right to left, and WS rows from left to right.

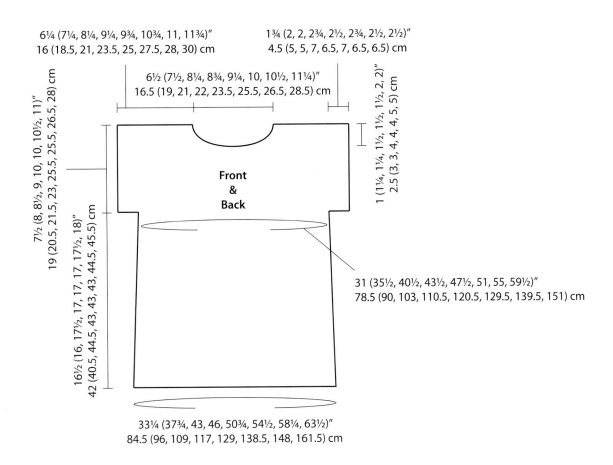

6¼ (7¼, 8¼, 9¼, 9¾, 10¾, 11, 11¾)"
16 (18.5, 21, 23.5, 25, 27.5, 28, 30) cm

1¾ (2, 2, 2¾, 2½, 2¾, 2½, 2½)"
4.5 (5, 5, 7, 6.5, 7, 6.5, 6.5) cm

6½ (7½, 8¼, 8¾, 9¼, 10, 10½, 11¼)"
16.5 (19, 21, 22, 23.5, 25.5, 26.5, 28.5) cm

1 (1¼, 1¼, 1½, 1½, 1½, 2, 2)"
2.5 (3, 3, 4, 4, 4, 5, 5) cm

7½ (8, 8½, 9, 10, 10, 10½, 11)"
19 (20.5, 21.5, 23, 25.5, 25.5, 26.5, 28) cm

**Front
&
Back**

16½ (16, 17½, 17, 17, 17, 17½, 18)"
42 (40.5, 44.5, 43, 43, 43, 44.5, 45.5) cm

31 (35½, 40½, 43½, 47½, 51, 55, 59½)"
78.5 (90, 103, 110.5, 120.5, 129.5, 139.5, 151) cm

33¼ (37¾, 43, 46, 50¾, 54½, 58¼, 63½)"
84.5 (96, 109, 117, 129, 138.5, 148, 161.5) cm

ZEPHYR

A study in serene comfort, Zephyr's pretty lace panels encourage the breeze. Cap sleeves and gentle princess shaping add finesse, while practical pockets keep life simple for the woman on the go. The silk and bamboo fiber blend offers the best of both worlds; a subtle sheen from the silk that elevates this tunic to a dressier level, and gorgeous, airy drape from the bamboo that will make it your go-to for a night out. Because it is worked from the top down, you can easily try on the tunic as you knit, ensuring the perfect fit.

SIZES

XS (S, M, L, XL, XXL, XXXL).
Finished bust circumference = 34½
(38, 40½, 44¾, 46¾, 48¾, 50¾)"
[87.5 (96.5, 103, 113.5, 118.5, 124,
129) cm]
Finished length (shoulder to bottom
edge) = 23¾ (24¾, 25, 26¼, 27, 27,
27¼)" [60.5 (63, 63.5, 66.5, 68.5,
68.5, 69) cm]

MATERIALS

Lorna's Laces Pearl [220 yds (201
m)/3.5oz (100 g)/, 51% silk, 49%
bamboo]. Color: The Skyway #1111.
4 (4, 4, 5, 5, 5, 5) skeins.
One US Size 6 (4 mm) 16" (40 cm),
24" (60 cm) and 32" (80 cm) long
circular needle, or size needed to
obtain gauge
Set of 4 or 5 US Size 6 (4 mm)
double-pointed needles (optional), or
size needed to obtain gauge
One set of 4 or 5 US Size 5 (3.75
mm) double-pointed needles for
pocket linings
Stitch markers (one in a unique color
for beg of rnd, three to mark body
shaping, and four in a third color to
indicate lace panels)
Tapestry needle
Waste yarn

GAUGE

20 sts and 26 rnds = 4" (10 cm) in
St st on larger needles, blocked.

PATTERN NOTES

Tunic is worked in one piece in the round from the top down, with pocket openings worked as you go. Lace instructions are provided in both written row-by-row and chart formats.

HAREBELL LACE: MULTIPLE OF 8 STS + 11

Rnd 1: K1, skp, yo, *k1, yo, s2kp, yo; rep from * to last 4 sts, k1, yo, k2tog, k1.
Rnd 2 and all even-numbered rnds: Knit.
Rnds 3 and 5: K1, skp, yo, *k5, yo, s2kp, yo; rep from * to last 8 sts, k5, yo, k2tog, k1.
Rnd 7: K3, *yo, skp, k1, k2tog, yo, k3; rep from * to end.
Rnd 8: Knit.

DIRECTIONS

YOKE

With shortest circ needle, CO 106 (108, 112, 114, 116, 118, 120) sts. Place unique marker for beg of rnd and join to work in the rnd, taking care not to twist sts.
Set-Up rnd: K17 for right sleeve, pm, k36 (37, 39, 40, 41, 42, 43) for front, pm, k17 for left sleeve, pm, k36 (37, 39, 40, 41, 42, 43) for back; rnds beg at right back raglan marker.
Next (inc) rnd: *K1 (raglan st), M1, knit to 1 st before next marker, M1, k1 (raglan st), sm; rep from * 3 times more. 8 sts increased.
Next Rnd: Purl.
Working in St st, rep inc rnd on next rnd, then every other rnd 5 (6, 6, 7, 7, 8, 8) more times, ending with an inc rnd. 152 (164, 168, 178, 180, 190, 192) sts; 29 (31, 31, 33, 33, 35, 35) sts for each sleeve, and 48 (51, 53, 56, 57, 60, 61) sts each for front and back. Change to longer circ needles as needed.
Next (set-up) rnd: Slipping markers as you come to them, *k29 (31, 31, 33, 33, 35, 35) sleeve sts, k2 (0, 1, 2, 3, 0, 1), pm in third color, work Harebell Lace over next 43 (51, 51, 51, 51, 59, 59) sts, pm in third color, k3 (0, 1, 3, 3, 1, 1); rep from * once more.
Rep inc rnd on next rnd, then every other rnd 15 (17, 19, 22, 24, 24, 26) more times, and AT THE SAME TIME work 15 more rnds in established lace patt.
Next rnd: Slipping markers as you come to them, *knit sleeve sts, k2 (0, 1, 2, 3, 0 1), work Harebell Lace over next 59 (67, 67, 67, 67, 75, 75) sts making sure each rep of st 10 lines up with st 6 of previous rnd (pattern shifts one-half rep to the right), k3 (0, 1, 3, 3, 1, 1); rep from * once more.
Work 7 more rnds as established, then continue in St st over all sts until raglan inc are complete. 282 (308, 328, 362, 380, 390, 408) sts; 61 (67, 71, 79, 83, 85, 91) sts for each sleeve, and 80 (87, 93, 102, 107, 110, 115) sts each for front and back.

DIVIDE FOR BODY AND SLEEVES

Next rnd: Removing raglan markers as you come to them, *place 61 (67, 71, 79, 83, 85, 91) sleeve sts on waste yarn for right sleeve. Using Backward Loop method, CO 3 (4, 4, 5, 5, 6, 6) sts, pm for side "seam," CO 3 (4, 4, 5, 5, 6, 6) more sts, k80 (87, 93, 102, 107, 110, 115) sts; rep from * once more, k3 (4, 4, 5, 5, 6, 6); rnd begins at right side "seam." [172 (190, 202, 224, 234, 244, 254) sts]

Next (set-up) rnd: *K18 (21, 22, 22, 23, 23, 24) of the front sts, pm for dart shaping, k50 (53, 57, 68, 71, 76, 79) sts, pm for dart shaping, k18 (21, 22, 22, 23, 23, 24) sts; rep from * once more. Work even in St st for 1½" [4 cm].

Shape Waist

Next (dec) rnd: *Knit to first marker, sm, ssk, knit to 2 sts before next marker, k2tog, sm; rep from * once more. 4 sts decreased.

[Rep dec rnd every 6th rnd 3 more times. 156 (174, 186, 208, 218, 228, 238) sts

Work even until body meas 6½ (6¼, 6, 6, 5¾, 5½)" [16.5 (16, 15, 15, 14.5, 14) cm] from underarm.

Next (inc) rnd: *Knit to first marker, sm, M1L, knit to next marker, M1R, sm, knit to side marker, sm; rep from * once more. 4 sts increased

Rep inc rnd every 5th rnd 4 more times. 176 (194, 206, 228, 238, 248, 258) sts

Knit 1 rnd even, removing dart markers.

Work even until body meas 9½ (9½, 9¼, 9¼, 9¼, 9, 8¾)" [24 (24, 23.5, 23.5, 23.5, 23, 22) cm] from underarm.

POCKETS

Next rnd: K9 (11, 12, 12, 13, 14, 15), sl next 22 (22, 22, 24, 24, 24, 24) sts onto waste yarn, use Backward Loop method to CO 22 (22, 22, 24, 24, 24, 24) sts over the gap, k26 (31, 35, 42, 45, 48, 51) sts, sl next 22 (22, 22, 24, 24, 24, 24) sts onto waste yarn, CO 22 (22, 22, 24, 24, 24, 24) sts over the gap, knit to end of rnd.

Next rnd: K9 (11, 12, 12, 13, 14, 15), p22 (22, 22, 24, 24, 24, 24) pocket sts, k26 (31, 35, 42, 45, 48, 51), p22 (22, 22, 24, 24, 24, 24) pocket sts, knit to end of rnd.

Next rnd: Knit.

Rep these two rnds once more. Work even in St st for 4" [10 cm].

Sizes S (XXXL) only

Knit 1 rnd and dec 2 sts evenly spaced. 192 (256) sts

Sizes M (L, XL) only

Knit 1 rnd and inc 2 (4, 2) sts evenly spaced. 208 (232, 240) sts

All sizes

Work 10 rnds of Harebell Lace patt, working 8-st rep only. Purl 1 rnd. Knit 1 rnd. Purl 1 rnd. BO all sts kwise.

SLEEVES (MAKE 2)

Place 61 (67, 71, 73, 79, 85, 91) held sleeve sts onto dpns or shortest circ needle. With RS facing, beg at center of underarm, pick up and k3 (4, 4, 5, 5, 6, 6) sts along underarm CO sts, knit sleeve sts, then pick up and k3 (4, 4, 5, 5, 6, 6) sts along underarm rem CO sts, pm for beg of rnd. 69 (75, 79, 83, 89, 97, 103) sts

Knit 2 rnds even. Purl 1 rnd. Knit 1 rnd. Purl 1 rnd. BO all sts knitwise.

FINISHING

Weave in loose ends. Block to measurements.

POCKET LININGS (MAKE 2)

Holding garment upside down, place 22 (22, 22, 24, 24, 24, 24) held pocket sts onto smaller dpn. Join yarn with RS facing. Work even in St st for 4" (10 cm), or until lining reaches last St st row before start of Harebell Lace border at bottom of body. Turn piece with WS of garment facing, use another dpn to pick up the 22 (22, 22, 24, 24, 24) sts directly below the pocket opening in the rnd above start of the border. With WS facing, hold dpns with sts just picked up and pocket lining sts tog and WS of lining facing you. Use 3-Needle BO to join pocket lining sts to sts just picked up. Sew sides of pocket lining to WS of body.

CHART KEY

- ☐ knit
- ☉ yo
- ◻ k2tog
- ◻ ssk
- ⊼ s2kp
- ☐ repeat

HAREBELL LACE

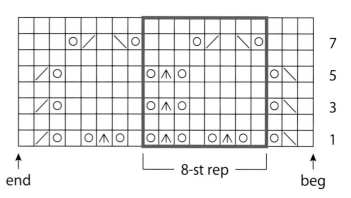

8-st rep

end   beg

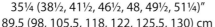

35¼ (38½, 41½, 46½, 48, 49½, 51¼)"
89.5 (98, 105.5, 118, 122, 125.5, 130) cm

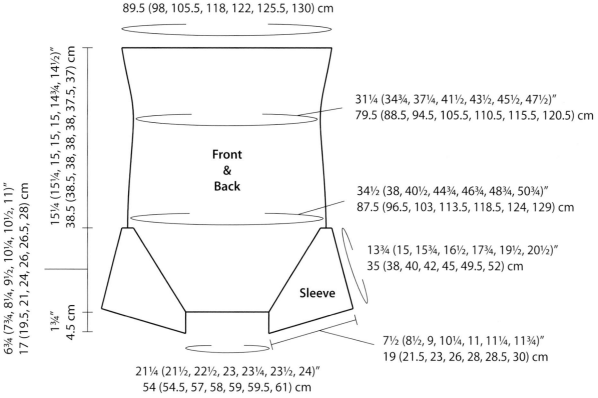

15¼ (15¼, 15, 15, 15, 14¾, 14½)"
38.5 (38.5, 38, 38, 38, 37.5, 37) cm

15¼ (15¼, 15, 15, 15, 14¾, 14½)"
38.5 (38.5, 38, 38, 38, 37.5, 37) cm

6¾ (7¾, 8¼, 9½, 10¼, 10½, 11)"
17 (19.5, 21, 24, 26, 26.5, 28) cm

1¾"
4.5 cm

Front
&
Back

Sleeve

31¼ (34¾, 37¼, 41½, 43½, 45½, 47½)"
79.5 (88.5, 94.5, 105.5, 110.5, 115.5, 120.5) cm

34½ (38, 40½, 44¾, 46¾, 48¾, 50¾)"
87.5 (96.5, 103, 113.5, 118.5, 124, 129) cm

13¾ (15, 15¾, 16½, 17¾, 19½, 20½)"
35 (38, 40, 42, 45, 49.5, 52) cm

7½ (8½, 9, 10¼, 11, 11¼, 11¾)"
19 (21.5, 23, 26, 28, 28.5, 30) cm

21¼ (21½, 22½, 23, 23¼, 23½, 24)"
54 (54.5, 57, 58, 59, 59.5, 61) cm

ABBREVIATIONS
AND TECHNIQUES

Approx	Approximately
Beg	Begin(ning)
BO	Bind off
CC	Contrast color
Circ	Circular needles
CO	Cast on
Cont	Continue(ing)
Dec	Decrease
Dpn	Double-pointed needles
Foll	Following
G	Gram(s)
Inc	Increase
K	Knit
K2tog	Knit 2 stitches together (decrease method)
K1f&b	Knit 1 through both front and back of the same stitch
LH	Left hand needle
MC	Main Color

M1L	Make 1 new stitch that slants left: Insert left needle from front to back into horizontal strand between the last stitch worked and the first stitch on left needle. Knit this strand through the back loop to twist it.
M1R	Make 1 new stitch that slants right: Insert left needle from back to front into horizontal strand between the last stitch worked and the next stitch on the left needle. Knit strand through the front loop to twist the stitch.
Oz	Ounce(s)
P	Purl
Patt	Pattern(s)
P2tog	Purl 2 stitches together
PB	(Place Bead)
Pm	Place marker
Psso	(pass slipped stitch over): Pass a slipped stitch over worked stitch(es)
Rem	Remain(ing)
Rnd(s)	Round(s)
Rep	Repeat
RH	Right hand needle

RS	Right side
Sl	Slip
Sl St	Slip stitch
Sk2p	Slip 1 stitch, knit next 2 stitches together, pass slipped stitch over knitted stitches
S2kp	Slip 2 stitches together as if to k2tog, knit next stitch, pass slipped stitches over decrease stitch
Sm	Slip marker
Ssk	Slip, slip, knit (decrease method): Slip 2 sts from LH to RH needle as if to purl, then knit both sts together.
St(s)	Stitch(es)
Tbl	Through back loop
Tog	Together
WS	Wrong side
W&t	(Wrap & turn): Short-row shaping method
Wyib	With yarn in back
Wyif	With yarn in front
Yo	Yarn over

*	Repeat directions following *
[ ]	Repeat directions inside brackets as many times as indicated

Please refer to my website, www.julieturjoman.com, for links to my favorite helpful tutorials on the following special techniques used in this book:

Backward Loop Cast-On
Cable Cast-On
Crochet Hook Method of Adding Beads
Make 1 Left and Make 1 Right Increases
Picot CO
Place Bead
Short-Row Shaping
Three-Needle Bind-Off

ACKNOWLEDGMENTS

No book is truly the work of a lone individual, and that is certainly the case with KNITS THAT BREATHE. As a card-carrying member of the knitting subculture, I embrace this wonderful community, and thank the overheated and wool-sensitive knitters whose laments inspired me to explore the world of plant-derived and alternative yarns.

This book would never have been possible without the generosity of several yarn companies: Berroco Inc., Blue Moon Fiber Arts, Classic Elite Yarns, Claudia Hand Painted Yarns, Handmaiden Yarns, Kolláge Yarn, Lorna's Laces, Prism Yarn, Shibui Knits, Sundara Yarn, and Valley Yarns. The kind folks at these companies supported my fascination with their traditional as well as their unconventional fibers, and encouraged my creative experiments by providing an array of gorgeous yarns.

I'm proud to be a member of Cat Bordhi's Visionaries, a cadre of intrepid self-publishing knitwear designers. For their advice, encouragement, and technical assistance, I am grateful.

Heartfelt thanks also go to:
Technical editor Therese Chynoweth, who whipped my patterns into shape with mathematical accuracy and stylistic consistency, ensuring that they can be easily understood and followed by everyone.

Glenna Eastwood, sample knitter extraordinaire, for her beautiful handwork.

Multi-talented book designer and artful photographer Zoë Lonergan, for her ability to understand exactly how I wanted this book to look and feel, and for her perfectionist's drive to make it that way.

Photo styling by the talented Katherine Yeh of StyleKouncil, and her industrious assistant, Brittany.

Friend and model Suzy Stemerman, whose beauty only grows with time, and whose expert knitting skills leave me in awe. Model Ashley Lonergan, who is graceful, stylish, and exceptionally good-natured.

Jane Davis, for her sharp editorial eye and equally sharp mind, her inspiring ability to overcome obstacles (knitting and otherwise), and for her welcoming friendship to this Chicago newbie.

Wendy Swords, my "sister from another mother," Chicago bestie, knitting enabler, fellow foodie, and sample knitting bacon-saver.

Tony and Rachel: you make it all possible, and you make it all worthwhile.

HERE'S WHERE YOU CAN FIND THE YARNS USED IN THIS BOOK...

BERROCO INC.
PO Box 367
14 Elmdale Rd.
Uxbridge, MA 01569
www.berroco.com
In Canada: S. R. Kertzer Ltd.
Linsey (Haven, p. 18)

BLUE MOON FIBER ARTS
56587 Mollenhour Rd
Scappoose, OR 97056
www.bluemoonfiberarts.com
Marine Silk Worsted (Sorbet, p. 66)

CLASSIC ELITE YARNS
122 Western Ave.
Lowell, MA 01851
www.classiceliteyarns.com
Seedling (Breezy, p. 4)

CLAUDIA HAND PAINTED YARNS
40 West Washington St.
Harrisonburg, VA 22802
www.claudiaco.com
Linen (Still Waters, p. 78)

HANDMAIDEN YARNS
Nova Scotia, Canada
www.handmaiden.ca
handmaiden@fleeceartist.com
Flaxen (Sirena, p. 58)

KOLLÁGE YARN
3591 Cahaba Beach Road
Birmingham, AL 35242

www.kollageyarns.com
Milky Whey (Iced Frappuccino, p. 26)

LORNA'S LACES
4229 N. Honore
Chicago, IL 60613
www.lornaslaces.net
Pearl (Zephyr, p. 84)
Sportmate (Sail Away, p. 52)

PRISM YARN
St. Petersburg, FL
www.prismyarn.com
Tencel Tape (Pacific Coast, p. 34)

SHIBUI KNITS, LLC
1500 NW 18th Suite 110
Portland, OR 97209
www.shibuiknits.com
Linen (Pochette, p. 42)

SUNDARA YARN
PO Box 1118
Carlsborg, WA 98324
www.sundarayarn.com
Silk Lace (Flutterbye, p. 12)

VALLEY YARNS
WEBS
75 Service Center Rd.
Northampton, MA 01060
www.yarn.com
Southwick (Splash, p. 72)

IF YOU WANT TO KNOW MORE...

Bernard, Wendy. *Custom Knits*. New York: STC Craft, 2008.

Budd, Ann. *The Knitter's Handy Book of Top-Down Sweaters*. Loveland, Colorado: Interweave Press, LLC, 2012.

Chin, Lily M. *Knit and Crochet with Beads*. Loveland, Colorado: Interweave Press, Inc., 2004.

Melville, Sally. *Knitting Pattern Essentials: Adapting and Drafting Knitting Patterns for Great Knitwear*. New York: Potter Craft, 2013.

Paden, Shirley. *Knitwear Design Workshop: A Comprehensive Guide to Handknits*. Loveland, Colorado: Interweave Press, LLC, 2009.

Parkes, Clara. *The Knitter's Book of Yarn: The Ultimate Guide to Choosing, Using, and Enjoying Yarn*. New York: Potter Craft, 2007.

Shroyer, Lisa. *Knitting Plus: Mastering Fit and Plus-Size Style*. Loveland, Colorado, Interweave Press, LLC, 2011.

Stanfield, Lesley and Melody Griffiths. *The Essential Stitch Collection*. Reader's Digest, 2010.

Editors of Vogue Knitting Magazine. *Vogue Knitting: the Ultimate Knitting Book*, New York: Sixth & Spring Books, 2002.

Walker, Barbara G. *A Treasury of Knitting Patterns*. Pittsville, WI: Schoolhouse Press, 1998.

Walker, Barbara G. *A Second Treasury of Knitting Patterns*. Pittsville, WI: Schoolhouse Press, 1998.

ABOUT THE AUTHOR

Julie Turjoman has been an accomplished knitter for more than 25 years. She is the author of **Brave New Knits: 26 Projects and Personalities From the Knitting Blogosphere** (New York, Rodale, Inc., 2010). In addition, her patterns have been published in *Interweave Knits*, *Jane Austen Knits*, *Knitty*, and *Twist Collective*, and have been included in the books **Vampire Knits** and **More Knitting In the Sun**.

She lives in Chicago, Illinois.

For more information, please visit:
www.julieturjoman.com